What People Are Saying A\
Releasing Spiritual Gifts Today...

James Goll's *Releasing Spiritual Gifts Today* is an excellent, well-written work. I like how he drew from different streams instead of just representing one stream or denominational viewpoint. James is a diligent student of the Word of God and the ways of God. His years of experience and years of study are reflected in this book. I love to be around bright people who are full of the Spirit and who value hearing from God. James was the first prophet whom I sat with and asked for prayer and activation in the prophetic. I sense God is readying the church for a new visitation. When He comes near, we experience more of His grace as empowerment through the expressions of grace seen in the gifts of the Holy Spirit. I sense this is the hour to no longer be satisfied with knowing about the grace gifts of God—God wants us to understand how to hear from Him and to act on His behalf through His divine enablements, His gifts. I am grateful to James for this labor of love that helps to clarify for many who are just now coming to the Master's banquet table the importance and the value of His gifts, and the way to begin flowing and growing in them.

—Randy Clark, D. Min.
Founder and president of Global Awakening and the
Apostolic Network of Global Awakening

In *Releasing Spiritual Gifts Today*, James Goll invites you to know and appreciate the gifts of the Spirit and to clearly understand what it means for you to release them. With solid biblical teaching, insights from noted Christian leaders, stirring testimonies, and personal application, he opens for you the realm of the supernatural where the movement of the Spirit is the norm, where people see the glory of God, and where healing and wholeness are restored to individuals and communities.

—Dr. Ché Ahn
Apostle, Harvest Apostolic Center, Pasadena, California
Senior pastor, HRock Church
President, Harvest International Ministry
International Chancellor, Wagner Leadership Institute

Dr. James Goll is one of the most thorough teachers in our day on subjects pertaining to the Spirit of God and kingdom life. His teachings are prophetically inspired, and yet any academically motivated individual will truly sit down to a feast when they use his materials and receive a prophetic infusion at the same time. The gifts of the Spirit is a subject dear to my heart as it was the first official training I received as a new believer. In his book, James does a brilliant job of empowering the hungry student in both understanding and activating these wonderful kingdom tools.

—*Patricia King*
Founder, XP Ministries
www.patriciaking.com

James Goll has been operating in the gifts of the Spirit for decades. Now, he's blending sound theology with practical experience to help you press into the supernatural in this valuable book. Whether you are a soccer mom who, as Paul admonishes us in 1 Corinthians 12:31, earnestly desires spiritual gifts or a minister who wants to root the operations of these gifts firmly in Scripture, *Releasing Spiritual Gifts Today* equips, inspires, and activates you to understand and press into the Holy Spirit's gifts. Every Christian needs to read this book!

—*Jennifer LeClaire*
Senior editor, *Charisma* magazine
Director, Awakening House of Prayer

James Goll's new book is a must for those who want to grow in the areas of hearing the voice of God and developing the gifts of the Spirit in their lives. I have had the honor of ministering with this dear man and observing him teach, impart, and activate others into their destiny. By reading this book, you will be activated in a supernatural anointing made natural in your life today!

—*Jerame Nelson*
Living At His Feet Ministries
Author, *Encountering Angels* and *Burning Ones*

I've always considered James Goll to be one of the main fathers of the modern-day prophetic movement. And just when I think he's exhausted what he might teach on the spiritual gifts today, he creates even better resources—including this book and its corresponding study guide, *Impacting the World Through Spiritual Gifts*—with the quality of university-level documentation. These works *have* to be the most comprehensive, best-documented materials on learning to both receive and operate in the biblical spiritual gifts available today. I daresay there is not a Scripture reference missing on the subject. Whether you are new to the subject or highly seasoned, you are about to discover a wealth of more biblical research than has ever before been at your fingertips!

—*Steve Shultz*
Founder, The Elijah List
Author, *Can You Speak Louder?*

James Goll is one of the most brilliant yet simple and down-to-earth leaders I know. We've been taught, taught, taught! Now James is rallying the call to release, release, release…spiritual gifts. *Releasing Spiritual Gifts Today* is so clear that releasing becomes simple. Just do it. And find someone to do it with. Releasing becomes contagious. This book will transform you into a DOER!

—*Barbara J. Yoder*
Lead Apostle, Shekinah Regional Apostolic Center, Ann Arbor, MI
Author, *The Breaker Anointing* and many other books

James Goll walks his talk and demonstrates what he teaches. I know this man and his teachings. We have served on each other's ministry boards for several years. James has given the body of Christ a great tool by presenting these spiritual truths in a manner that is understandable and yet filled with a depth of Scripture/historical precedent mixed with modern-day examples. If you believe that Jesus Christ is the same, yesterday, today and forever, then you are going to love *Releasing Spiritual Gifts Today!*

—*Elizabeth Alves*
Founder, Increase International
International best-selling author, *Mighty Prayer Warrior*

Natural ability and talents are great and are God-given. But your natural talents aren't enough to fulfill the divine purpose and calling God has for you. You need the anointing and operation of the Holy Spirit to be able to do all God has called you to do. *Releasing Spiritual Gifts Today* by James Goll will empower you to operate in a new level of spiritual gifting and power! In this book, James Goll masterfully teaches on the subject of functioning in all nine gifts of the Holy Spirit, including the gifts of revelation, power, and utterance. He teaches in a clear, organized, and powerful way. Not only will you learn what the gifts of the Spirit are, but you will also learn practical steps to seeing these manifestations of God increase in and through you. You will be equipped to impact the lives of those around you with the power of the Holy Spirit. I highly recommend this book for individuals, home groups, churches, Bible studies, and Bible schools. It will be a great resource in your spiritual arsenal!

—*Matt Sorger*
Prophetic healing revivalist
TV host and author, *Power for Life*
mattsorger.com

RELEASING SPIRITUAL *Gifts* TODAY

JAMES W. GOLL

WHITAKER
HOUSE

Boldface type in the Scripture quotations indicates the author's emphasis.

RELEASING SPIRITUAL GIFTS TODAY

James W. Goll
Encounters Network
P.O. Box 1653
Franklin, TN 37065
www.encountersnetwork.com • www.prayerstorm.com
www.compassionacts.com • www.GETeSchool.com
info@encountersnetwork.com • inviteJames@gmail.com

ISBN: 978-1-62911-604-4
eBook ISBN: 978-1-62911-605-1
Printed in the United States of America
© 2016 by James W. Goll

Whitaker House
1030 Hunt Valley Circle
New Kensington, PA 15068
www.whitakerhouse.com

Library of Congress Cataloging-in-Publication Data

Title: Releasing spiritual gifts today / James W. Goll.
Description: New Kensington, PA : Whitaker House, 2016. | Includes bibliographical references.
Identifiers: LCCN 2015048492 (print) | LCCN 2015049517 (ebook) | ISBN 9781629116044 (trade pbk. : alk. paper) | ISBN 9781629116051 (E-book)
Subjects: LCSH: Gifts, Spiritual.
Classification: LCC BT767.3 .G65 2016 (print) | LCC BT767.3 (ebook) | DDC 234/.13—dc23
LC record available at http://lccn.loc.gov/2015048492

3 4 5 6 7 8 9 10 11 12 **WH** 23 22 21 20 19 18

CONTENTS

ACKNOWLEDGMENTS AND DEDICATION

Releasing Spiritual Gifts Today has been developed from the gleanings of the ministries of others. Over the years, I have endeavored to be a student of many of the different streams of the movements of the Holy Spirit that have flowed through the church of Jesus Christ. These pages reflect that study.

In particular, I want to acknowledge the friendship and ministry of Mahesh and Bonnie Chavda, who have given me so much. I learned a great deal about the gift of discerning of spirits through Pat Gastineau of Word of Love in Roswell, Georgia, and I was exposed to the gift of faith through the late Kenneth Hagin, as well as other spiritual pioneers. I thank the Lord for the teaching ministry of Jim Croft, the groundbreaking exploration of signs and wonders of John Wimber, and the apostolic teaching first of Derek Prince and then of C. Peter Wagner.

In the pages that follow, I acknowledge the contributions of several of these friends who have written books on the topic of spiritual gifts, along with Sam Storms, Dick Iverson, and Mel Robeck. I have also benefited greatly from the prophetic impartations of John Sanford, Cindy Jacobs, Bill Hamon, the late Bob Jones, and several others.

First and foremost, I am thankful to our Father for sending us the precious Holy Spirit, the third person of the Godhead, who is our greatest gift! Therefore, with a grateful heart, I dedicate this book to the work and ministry of the Holy Spirit. You are our Comforter, our Guide, our Fruit-bearer, and our Gift-bringer. Come, Holy Spirit, and empower Your people anew!

FOREWORD

The Holy Spirit is doing great things in our day! The authentic, supernatural activity of the Holy Spirit is on the increase all around the world. In these last days, the Holy Spirit is actively preparing the bride of Messiah for her Bridegroom King. These are the most exciting days to be alive!

As the host of the international television program *It's Supernatural!*, it is part of my calling and job description to be exposed to the activity of the Holy Spirit today. I honor all that God has done in the past, but I have my gaze set on what He is doing today while anticipating a great increase in the demonstration of the gifts of the Holy Spirit tomorrow.

Most books on the supernatural are about supernatural gifts that operate in the author's life or how the gifts themselves function. I rejoice over them, but books of that nature don't interest me. What interests me is a book that teaches me *how to release* the gifts. That brings me to James Goll, a friend of God and an instructor in the ways of God today. Ever since my friend James was set on fire by the Holy Spirit, he has been a demonstrator of the grace and power of God's Spirit. Now, for the first time, he teaches the field-tested secrets he has learned so that you can release the gifts of the Spirit in your life.

We are in the last of the last days. Jesus is coming back soon. Now is the time for you, too, to experience the fire of the Holy Spirit and to operate in the gifts. If not now, when? This unique book is not only scripturally sound but also filled with testimonies of the Holy Spirit's work today. So buckle your seat belt, because you are going to learn to soar higher than ever before!

—*Sid Roth*

PREFACE:
JUST DO IT!

I have intentionally titled this book *Releasing Spiritual Gifts Today* rather than "Receiving Spiritual Gifts" because I believe we should *do* something with spiritual gifts now—not just study them in order to learn what they are and how to obtain them. Giving God's love to others by means of His gifts presupposes first having received them, and it is important to learn how to use the gifts of His Spirit today rather than merely learn how to receive them and then sit on our hands and do nothing with them!

Not long ago, "the gifts of the Holy Spirit" was a hot topic, and most of the books about spiritual gifts that are available were published in the recent past. Yet even though you will not hear as much preaching and teaching about them these days, God has not rescinded His gifts or His commissioning. He has not lifted these special manifestations of His grace. Rather, in these latter days that we are living in, He has determined to pour them forth *all the more*, with even greater degrees of impact and authority. God not only wants you to learn about His gifts, but He also wants you to experience the great wonder of moving in and through His grace on a daily basis. Experience, under the direction of the Holy Spirit, will be your best tutor; and you can expect to keep learning as you keep on doing—today, tomorrow, and the next day. Practice does make perfect! As the popular slogan goes, "Just do it!"

THE NINE MOST WIDELY RECOGNIZED GIFTS

Releasing Spiritual Gifts Today is divided into four parts, with three chapters in each section. The first section gives you an overview of spiritual gifts and introduces you to the way the Holy Spirit moves and operates through them. Sections two through four give you specific information about the nine most widely recognized spiritual gifts, grouped together as "Revelatory Gifts," "Power Gifts," and "Vocal Gifts."

Section two, "Revelatory Gifts," describes three gifts that "reveal": discerning of spirits, word of wisdom, and word of knowledge. Section three, "Power Gifts," examines three gifts that "do": faith, healings, and workings of miracles. Last, but not least, "Vocal Gifts" covers three gifts that "speak," or gifts that rely on the human vocal cords for manifestation: tongues, interpretation of tongues, and prophecy. These nine gifts are not the only gifts God gives to His children, but they are vital ones to learn about, to understand, and to activate as He leads.

Throughout, I give you plenty of examples of these spiritual gifts in action, both in current, everyday life and within the pages of the Bible. It is always exciting to see God working through His people; and even when we revisit familiar biblical stories, we can always see something new in them.

INFORMATION, INSPIRATION, AND IMPARTATION

My three main purposes for this book are *information*, *inspiration*, and *impartation*. First, that the information presented here will bring you into a greater awareness of biblical truth about spiritual gifts. Second, that you will be inspired, through the personal and biblical stories, to greater levels of hope and faith regarding the tremendous potential of the gifts God has given to you. Third, that you will be imparted by the Spirit with the courage to step forward and use them.

It is my hope that all of us will study to show ourselves approved as effective workers for our Master. (See 2 Timothy 2:15.) The Lord has gifted each and every one of us. May He be magnified in our lives as we serve as His hands and feet and voice in the world around us.

Nothing will happen if you don't step out in faith. Let the words you are about to read stir you to respond anew to His direction so that you can "just do it"––use the spiritual gifts that God gives you—every day of your life. Remember, faith is spelled R-I-S-K, and the best fruit is always way out there on the end of the limb! What does the Lord want to do for you and through you? Let's turn the page and see what He has in store for you today.

SECTION ONE

INTRODUCTION TO SPIRITUAL GIFTS

*I*n this section, I introduce you to the broad subject of the Holy Spirit and spiritual gifts. I explain the basis for exercising spiritual gifts today, because there are some people who believe that these gifts, which were used by believers in the early church, have ceased. *Cessationism* is the idea that all "signs and wonders" spiritual gifts ceased after the lifetimes of the original apostles, including the apostle Paul. Cessationist ideas are still embraced in this generation. However, they are not as influential as they once were because church history and present-day manifestations of the Holy Spirit easily refute such a doctrine. A rising tide of millions of people have been touched by the Holy Spirit in recent decades, and they have experienced His power and the manifestation of His gifts.

Instead of cessationism, I believe in "continue-ism." God has not rescinded His gifts or His commissioning! He continues to pour out His Holy Spirit upon His people, as on the day of Pentecost, to bless His people and to reach the world with His love and truth.

In chapter 1, we discuss the question "What are spiritual gifts?" and see how the Holy Spirit is the author of all spiritual gifts.

In chapter 2, we discover and understand how the Holy Spirit moves. As I say in that chapter, it is not always easy to track with a Spirit who comes and goes like an invisible breeze. But we can depend on His promises to help us follow Him and learn His ways. He stretches us beyond ourselves, moving us to testify of the love and power of God and showing us how to bear fruit that lasts. Chapter 2 provides keys for getting to know the Holy Spirit. Because He lives inside us, we can lean into Him, walk with Him, live with Him, and listen to Him. We can depend on Him to always lead us out of darkness and into the light.

In chapter 3, we explore how to exercise spiritual gifts. Yes, I said "exercise." It takes practice, lots of practice, to become mature in the use of spiritual gifts. The Holy Spirit is at work everywhere in the world. This means that all of His gifts are still fully operational. I emphasize that the word is *operational*, not "optional," and that any and all of God's children are supposed to be using them. As John Wimber put it, spiritual gifts are *tools*. They are not toys. You need to practice using them, and you will not be an expert on your first try.

The gifts of the Spirit are meant to be used by believers to touch the world with the kingdom of God. Empowered and enabled by Him, we can do signs and wonders in the marketplace, on the street, in the grocery store parking lot, at Starbucks—wherever. I believe that the gifts of the Spirit are as expansive as God Himself, so there is no reason to adhere rigidly to a particular set or listing of them. The exciting thing is that, in our lifetimes, we can expect to see the darkness overcome by unprecedented, brilliant displays of God's grace and supernatural power—through His gifted people, as we preach the salvation message of Jesus Christ.

1

WHAT ARE THE SPIRITUAL GIFTS?

"To each is given the manifestation of the Spirit for the common good."
—1 Corinthians 12:7 (esv)

I had an opportunity to travel around the country of Albania for several weeks, right after Communism was lifted there in 1992, teaching leaders in several cities about the present-day ministry of the Holy Spirit. The territory of Albania overlaps that of ancient Illyricum, a Roman province where Paul preached and actively showed the people the power of the Spirit. We know about Paul's ministry there from his letter to the Roman church:

> *Therefore in Christ Jesus I have found reason for boasting in things pertaining to God. For I will not presume to speak of anything except what Christ has accomplished through me, resulting in the obedience of the Gentiles by word and deed, in the power of signs and wonders, in*

the power of the Spirit; so that from Jerusalem and round about as far as Illyricum I have fully preached the gospel of Christ.

(Romans 15:17–20)

One of the cities in Albania where I held meetings is called Shëngjin, which is Albanian for "St. John," and their tradition holds that Paul once preached there, in addition to Titus and John the Beloved. As it turned out, I was part of the first public meeting in recent history at which the gospel would be preached, accompanied by signs and wonders in the power of the Spirit. Only God could have set things up so well to confirm the truth of the gospel.

There was no church building for our meeting, so we gathered in a fortress-like community building on a cold, rainy February evening. There were maybe a hundred and twenty people packed into the room, all wearing their winter coats because it was as bitterly cold inside the place as it was outside. I had to make do without much support; I didn't even have a worship team or a source of worship music. Except for my Christian interpreter and the friend who came with me, everybody else in the room spoke *shqip* (pronounced roughly like "shkeep"), which is the Albanian language. I had been praying specifically for a word from God for these spiritually hungry people who had gone for so long without one. Through my interpreter, I began to preach about how God sets us free from rejection and oppression, and I told a little bit about my background and testimony.

After I launched into my sermon, I kept speaking for a while, although I could see I wasn't getting much of anywhere. Then the name *Sarah* floated through my mind. That was the second time it had happened that day. Earlier, as I had been preparing myself in prayer for the meeting, the same name had occurred to me. I had put it aside because I felt I was supposed to minister to the whole group, not just to one person; and anyway, I had reasoned, Sarah is not an Albanian name.

But now that the name had been brought to my attention a second time, I had to assume that God had given it to me for a reason. I turned to my interpreter and asked, "What is the name 'Sarah' in Albanian?"

"Sabrina," he said.

"Is anyone here named Sabrina?" I asked. A youngish lady with a somber expression raised her hand. Everyone seemed to know her. I asked her to step out into the aisle and to come forward, which she did, bundled in her coat. Only then did I start to grasp more of what to say to her. I prophesied, and my words were translated for her as I said, "Your name is Sabrina. You have never heard the gospel of the Lord Jesus Christ ever in your life. You are thirty-two years old. You have a tumor in your left breast, and Jesus wants to heal you."

The woman looked startled at my words. She had never before been to a Christian meeting, especially not to a charismatic-type meeting. Yet even without ever having seen it happen before, she began to tremble violently. She knew the words were true. The rest of the people knew it, too, because they knew her. Sabrina gave her heart to Jesus in front of the group, followed by others. Even those who may not have been saved that night definitely had an encounter with the power of the living God. That evening, we all forgot about being cold, because God's presence was so intense.

Eventually things settled down, and everyone went home except for the three of us: my friend, my interpreter, and me. We didn't have a hotel or a home nearby to go to; we were supposed to travel to the next city, where we were lodging. The security guard escorted us down the hill to the street, where we hoped to be able to hail a taxicab, although cars were scarce in all of Albania, and the roads were terrible. All we could do in the rainy, dark night (no streetlights, either) was to try to thumb a ride.

Amazingly, a car pulled over. It crossed my mind that this was like the incident in the book of Acts where Philip got into the Ethiopian official's chariot—and God got in, too. (See Acts 8:26–40.) The driver was willing to take us to the next city, so we got into his "chariot," and our God-sent chauffeur set out, navigating around the potholes in the dark.

I occupied the front passenger seat, with my interpreter and my friend in the back. The interpreter translated for me as I started telling the guy the story of what had just happened at the community center. All of a sudden, the driver was seized with trembling, and it wasn't because of the bad road; it became clear to me that I was in the middle of another divine appointment. This man turned out to be Sabrina's husband! He was a Muslim, and he had never heard the gospel before, either. He kept driving, and I kept talking. Before we arrived at our destination, he was saved, too, by the power of the Holy Spirit.

After that, I knew I could make Paul's words to the Corinthians my own: *"My message and my preaching were not in persuasive words of wisdom, but in demonstration of the Spirit and of power"* (1 Corinthians 2:4). God was doing a mighty work in northern Albania!

GIFTS FOR TODAY

You may not hear about that sort of thing happening very frequently in your immediate neighborhood, but it is a fact that the Holy Spirit is demonstrating God's power through His church much more widely than we realize. The Spirit is at work everywhere in the world, and *"Jesus Christ is the same yesterday and today and forever"* (Hebrews 13:8). This means that all of His gifts are still fully operational, such as the prophetic gift through which I was given the word for Sabrina.

I said that the gifts are *operational*, not "optional," and all of God's children should be using them. You and I—every single believer—are supposed to have at least one manifestation of the Spirit functioning in our lives. We have been equipped to do the same things the disciples did in the book of Acts—signs and wonders and everything in between. We are not to be ignorant of our gifts; we are expected to learn about them. (See, for example, 1 Corinthians 12:1, 4–11; 1 Peter 4:10–11.)

"DOIN' THE STUFF!"

The late John Wimber, who was well-known as a teacher and a leader in the Vineyard movement, coined the phrase "Doin' the stuff!" to refer to all of the displays of God's power, wherever and whenever they occur, that augment the preaching of the gospel and the spreading of the good news of the kingdom. Wimber also said,

Spiritual gifts are the expression of God's power at work in the Church today. A believer does not possess gifts; a believer receives gifts from God to be used at special times for special occasions. Gifts are the attestation of the empowering of the Holy Spirit and are vital in a "signs and wonders" ministry.

Spiritual empowering equips one for service. The gifts are the tools which enable one to fulfill the ministry required.

The gifts of the Spirit are received by impartation. The gifts (except the private use of tongues) are given to us and through us to use for others, and are developed in a climate of risk-taking and willingness to fail.[1]

Spiritual gifts are not ours to simply play with—or not—according to our own whims. They are ours to activate by faith and to use at God's direction. Whenever He wants to bring His kingdom to bear on something, His first choice is to use a spiritual-gift-equipped follower. That man or woman or child does not have to be a "professional religious person," as I happen to be, which is why I was invited to Albania. God could have engineered the situation so that someone else's spiritual gifts were the ones that came into play there, as He typically uses the nearest available believer to accomplish His purposes throughout the world.

WHAT ARE SPIRITUAL GIFTS?

As John Wimber put it, spiritual gifts are *tools*; they are not toys. As such, you need to practice using them, and you will not be an expert on your first try. It is no small thing to step out in public to use them. You really do have to be willing to appear stupid and to fail. Nothing is guaranteed, except that the Holy Spirit will be with you. John Wimber, for example, became convinced that God wanted to use him to pray for the sick. First, he learned everything he could about gifts of healings. Then he began to try it out. He prayed for at least a hundred people before one person got healed. It must have been discouraging, not to mention embarrassing. But he kept at it, because he was convinced that God's gifts of healings were meant for today, and that healings should be occurring wherever the gospel is being proclaimed. As he prayed for the second hundred people, two were healed. He kept getting more and more experience and gaining more and more faith, and the numbers of those who were healed kept increasing accordingly. Eventually, miraculous healing was a major component of his ministry.

In the same way, we need to be willing to practice the gifts purposefully as we learn from spiritual mentors and become willing to take risks. The Holy Spirit will never impel you to do something. If you are waiting for the "dancing hand of God"[2] to overcome you and cause you to say or to do something, you will wait forever. You need to act.

To give a thorough scriptural grounding for his definition of spiritual gifts, John Wimber quoted Mel Robeck, who is on the faculty at Fuller Theological Seminary:

> The gifts (*charismata*) of the Holy Spirit are the transrational [going beyond human reason] manifestations of God. They are given by God for the purpose of ministry taking place for the good of the Body of Christ (1 Corinthians 12:7).
>
> The *source* of the gifts is the Holy Spirit (1 Corinthians 12; Hebrews 2:4).
>
> The *recipients* are the community of the Spirit, sometimes called the people of God or the Body of Christ (1 Corinthians 12; Romans 12; Ephesians 4; 1 Peter 4:10–11).
>
> Their *purpose* is to edify the Body, equip the saints, and glorify God.
>
> Their *motive* should always be love (1 Corinthians 13:1–13).
>
> The way and wherefore of spiritual gifts is directly related to the work of the Holy Spirit throughout history.[3]

This last point, about the Holy Spirit's working throughout history, stands in direct contradiction to the belief of much of the Western church that the "signs and wonders" gifts of the Holy Spirit disappeared with the last of the original apostles. This view is called *cessationism*. But when you have had experiences such as I had in Albania with Sabrina and her husband, it is difficult to hang on to cessationist ideas. I wrote this book in part to underline my conviction that *cessationism will cease*. The idea that the gifts have ceased will cease! The gifts of the Holy Spirit are alive and well in countless Christians today. If you are not yet one of them, I hope that you will be by the time you finish this book.

ARE SPIRITUAL GIFTS HUMAN ABILITIES?

We must realize that the gifts of the Spirit are not just human talents and abilities, polished until they shine with God's light. Although humans do use their innate, God-given faculties when they use the gifts of the Spirit as tools, the gifts are not part of their original "tool set." We can observe that God employs and strengthens human temperaments and abilities by His Spirit, but that is not the same thing as receiving spiritual gifts, which are "direct manifestations of the Holy Spirit through believers."[4]

Apostolic teacher and prolific author Peter Wagner summarized the nature and purpose of spiritual gifts in this way: "A spiritual gift is a special attribute given by the Holy Spirit to every member of the Body of Christ, according to God's grace, for use within the context of the Body."[5] His phrase "within the context of the Body" does not mean that spiritual gifts are to be used only within the church. They are to be used by the members of the body of Christ anywhere and everywhere, as God determines—which ends up putting any situation into the "context" of the body.[6]

The late international Bible teacher Derek Prince wrote that "no believer in Jesus Christ needs to be without his own distinctive manifestation of the Holy Spirit."[7] The gifts of the Spirit are meant to be used by believers to touch the world with the kingdom of God. Empowered and enabled by Him, we can do signs and wonders in the marketplace, on the street, in the grocery store parking lot, at Starbucks, and so on. Both inside and outside the community of believers, we can heal the sick, do prophetic evangelism, and more.

WHY DOES GOD GIVE SPIRITUAL GIFTS?

For the Common Good

Scripture exhorts us to seek spiritual gifts (see 1 Corinthians 12:31; 14:1), and the apostle Paul made it clear that the gifts are meant to be used on behalf of other people:

But to each one is given the manifestation of the Spirit for the common good. For to one is given the word of wisdom through the Spirit, and to another the word of knowledge according to the same Spirit; to another faith by the same Spirit, and to another gifts of healing by the one Spirit, and to another the effecting of miracles, and to another prophecy, and to another the distinguishing ["discerning" NKJV] of spirits, to another various kinds of tongues, and to another the interpretation of tongues. But one and the same Spirit works all these things, distributing to each one individually just as He wills.

(1 Corinthians 12:7–11)

Each of us has been gifted for the sake of others. Further on in his first letter to the Corinthian church, Paul said, *"Pursue love, yet desire earnestly spiritual gifts"* (1 Corinthians 14:1), and *"Even so you, since you are zealous for spiritual gifts, let it be for the edification of the church that you seek to excel"* (1 Corinthians 14:12 NKJV).

A lot of people miss this point. They get their identities all wrapped up in their giftedness when their identities should be wrapped up in Christ Jesus. God's gifts to you are never a statement about how much He loves you. It is easy to think this way, particularly when God does something sensational through you. You almost can't help but feel that it proves God's special favor, but it doesn't. When we look at Jesus' life, we see Someone whose internal security did not rest on earning a high approval rating from His Father, Someone who served in various capacities over His lifetime, many of them unspectacular. In a similar way, each one of us will serve many different functions over the course of our lives, and most of the time, we will be out of the public eye. We will move around from place to place and have various spheres of influence. Our relationships will change, and the use of our giftings may shift to match the needs of our situation. But if we are fixed on God and not on the gifts He gives us, we can remain stable and secure in any situation.

Some people are like shooting stars; they rise in a hurry but burn out quickly. I want to be fixed, like the North Star, unshakeable and strong because God is unshakeable and strong. As we fix our eyes on Him, we can hold on to the fact that once God gives a gift, it will not be withdrawn or recalled. What He gives, He does not take back. (See Romans 11:29.) We can rest in that truth and not try to run ahead of God's plans for us.

What it comes down to is that spiritual gifts are more about how much God wants to love other people through you than how much He loves you (even though He does, indeed, love you!). You are a channel of His grace. The gifts have been given to you so you can channel His love to someone else. Gifts are for giving away!

For the Whole Body

The gifts operate similarly to the functioning of the human body, where each part and organ works together with the others so the whole body can flourish. (See 1 Corinthians 12:12–31; Romans 12:4–8.) God gives spiritual gifts so that the entire body of Christ can profit from them, so that each member can benefit the other members of the body. The body of Christ is not just a gathering of individual believers—it is organic; it is the living body of the Lord Jesus Christ on earth today, demonstrating God's grace. *"Now you are Christ's body, and individually members of it"* (1 Corinthians 12:27).

Too often, a church body comes together based on people's common interests, passions, desires, or talents. But God intended for us to group ourselves according to gifts so that we could learn from one another and then give to the other parts of the body, and eventually from the body to the whole world.

Each of us has been gifted for the sake of others. The nine gifts that I will be describing in detail in this book are not the totality of body ministry, but total body ministry is not possible without them.

For the Effectiveness of the Gospel

It is impossible to have a glorious, fully functioning body of Christ apart from the *charismata*, the gifts of the Spirit. Without supernatural endowments, the church cannot presume to preach the gospel to the whole world and to reap the great harvest prior to the coming of the Lord. (See Matthew 24:14.) Another way of saying it is that the gospel is not being fully preached unless it is *"with signs following"* (Mark 16:20 KJV).

When the early disciples were scattered by persecution, they took the gospel wherever they went:

> Those who had been scattered went about preaching the word. Philip went down to the city of Samaria and began proclaiming Christ to them. The crowds with one accord were giving attention to what was said by Philip, as they heard and saw the signs which he was perform- ing. For in the case of many who had unclean spirits, they were coming out of them shouting with a loud voice; and many who had been para- lyzed and lame were healed. So there was much rejoicing in that city.
>
> (Acts 8:4–8)

When was the last time you witnessed such signs? We are still living in New Testament times today, and we should be looking to God to give us the gifts that bring about convincing signs and wonders so that a dying world can be introduced to the true Life from heaven, Jesus Christ. Jesus Himself said that supernatural gifts would be the "credentials" of believers. (See Mark 16:17–20; Acts 4:33; Hebrews 2:3–4.)

HOW TO RECEIVE GOD'S GRACES AND GIFTS

Very well, we know that God wants to give us gifts so that we can ben- efit the other members of the body of Christ and spread the good news of the kingdom. But how does He do this? And how can we activate our faith to receive His gifts and to exercise them—here and now? The following are steps for positioning ourselves receptively as we seek God and His gifts.

1. Choose God's Choice for You

First, we choose God's choice for us. You are probably aware of the theological tension within the church between God's sovereignty and hu- man free will. Without addressing the controversy in detail, let us acknowl- edge that God is sovereign over all and that He gives us graces, ministries, and spiritual offices as He desires; His decision to bestow gifts is not de- pendent on the recipient's preparation or choosing. It is God's election, and we do not get to vote on it. (See, for example, Acts 2:1–4; 10:44–46.)

Yet, although God chooses our gift, we get to choose His choice for us. It is like the pedals of a bicycle. When one is up, the other is down, and they bring each other round and round. It takes pressure first on one, then the other, to make the bike roll forward. In the same way, it takes these two seemingly opposed truths joining forces to reach the goal of receiving and exercising spiritual gifts. Is it God's sovereignty? Or our free will? Yes—both.

Let us choose to receive and operate in the gifts God has for us.

2. Be Open and Receptive to God

After choosing God's will, we need to actively seek and ask for what God has chosen, making ourselves available to receive it. Those who are already gifted can help each other to receive God's gifts, often through the laying on of hands. We see this practice throughout the history of the people of God, especially after the Holy Spirit was given to the church. One example in the Old Testament is when Moses laid his hands on Joshua to impart to him the gift of leadership: *"Now Joshua the son of Nun was filled with the spirit of wisdom, for Moses had laid his hands on him; and the sons of Israel listened to him and did as the LORD had commanded Moses"* (Deuteronomy 34:9). This impartation would not have occurred without Joshua first being willing to receive it.

In the New Testament, both divine sovereignty and human free will were involved in the outpouring of the Holy Spirit on the disciples in the upper room on the day of Pentecost. None of the believers there could have caused the wind of the Spirit to blow or the tongues of fire to appear in the air over their heads. But, obedient to the word Jesus had given them, they had waited together patiently and expectantly for God's gift. Jesus had *"commanded them not to leave Jerusalem, but to wait for what the Father had promised, 'Which,' He said, 'you heard of from Me; for John baptized with water, but you will be baptized with the Holy Spirit not many days from now'"* (Acts 1:4–5). The believers postured themselves receptively, praying and worshipping, not really knowing what God was going to give them but willing to receive it. Then, once they were filled with the Spirit, they voluntarily allowed their tongues to be loosened and their voices to speak out new sounds *"as the Spirit was giving them utterance"* (Acts 2:4).

Nobody laid hands on anybody else on the day of Pentecost, but the disciples often used this practice afterward as they figured out how God wanted things to be done within the body of people who would be called the church. God wanted everyone to be filled with His Spirit, and He equipped the believers with the character and the wisdom necessary to make good decisions about methods and timing. For example, Paul told Timothy not to be "hasty" in the laying on of hands, but rather to use wisdom, so that the will of God could be achieved without being compromised by human sinfulness. (See 1 Timothy 5:22.)

Look at this sampling of the New Testament practice of the laying on of hands for commissioning in ministry:

They had these men [Stephen and others who had been chosen to oversee the daily distribution of food to poor widows] *stand before the apostles, who prayed and laid their hands on them.*　　(Acts 6:6 NRSV)

So Ananias went and entered the house. He laid his hands on Saul [Paul] *and said, "Brother Saul, the Lord Jesus, who appeared to you on your way here, has sent me so that you may regain your sight and be filled with the Holy Spirit."*　　(Acts 9:17 NRSV)

While they [the leaders of the church at Antioch] *were worshiping the Lord and fasting, the Holy Spirit said, "Set apart for me Barnabas and Saul for the work to which I have called them." Then after fasting and praying they laid their hands on them and sent them off.*
(Acts 13:2–3 ESV)

Sometimes, the laying on of hands confers an impartation of great magnitude, such as with Ananias and Paul. An impartation can also occur without the laying on of hands, as in the case of intentional mentoring. Sometimes we call this "casting a mantle," in reference to the way the prophet Elijah's actual mantle, his anointed piece of clothing, was cast over the shoulders of Elisha, who became his successor. (See 1 Kings 19:16, 19.) That simple act determined the course of the rest of Elisha's life. He became Elijah's servant and learned how to operate in God's giftings. Finally, at the end of Elijah's life, Elisha became the sole possessor of the mantle that had once been put over his shoulders (see 2 Kings 2:1–14), and he went on to perform even more miraculous prophetic acts than his mentor Elijah had.

Does God impart His gifts any less today? Shouldn't we rather expect more activity of the Holy Spirit now, as the last days unfold? Sometimes, if I don't have anybody who can pray for me, I lay hands on myself in order to stir up the gifts that God wants to use. I lay my hands on my stomach and say, "Out of my innermost being will come forth rivers of living water" (see John 7:38)—and it works! The gifts He has given me flow forth for the sake of other people. In fact, one of the greatest joys in my life is to see people have God-encounters! It is better than watching a great movie. You and I get to be the actors on God's stage in the "Greatest Show on Earth"!

3. Make Yourself Available to God

We should be aware that it is quite possible to miss our chance to receive an impartation of God's grace. I remember seeing the healing evangelist Kathryn Kuhlman on a television broadcast late in her life. "I was not God's first choice," she confided. "God offered this gift, this ministry, to a man first. And he refused. So then God came to an ugly woman with red hair and freckles...and I said yes." She received the gift and the call because she made herself available.

Think about how Jesus' disciples received His impartations. They made themselves available when He called them and sent them out to minister in His authority. Out into the countryside they went, without Him, to test their new gifts, and then they came back to report their successes to Him. (See, for example, Luke 10:1–11, 17–19.) "Doin' the stuff" brought them great joy, even in the midst of the personal sacrifices and difficulties that came with the territory.

A MULTIPLICITY OF GIFTS

For the purposes of this book, I have chosen to concentrate on nine of the most important gifts of the Spirit, which are found in 1 Corinthians 12: discerning of spirits, a word of wisdom, a word of knowledge, faith, gifts of healings, tongues, interpretation of tongues, prophecy, and workings of miracles. But Scripture presents a number of other spiritual gifts. Look at this wonderful inventory of gifts, listed alphabetically, which includes the nine gifts I have just mentioned:

1. Administrations, or "steerings" (see 1 Corinthians 12:28)
2. Apostle (see 1 Corinthians 12:28; Ephesians 4:11)
3. Celibacy (see 1 Corinthians 7:7)
4. Discerning (or distinguishing) of spirits (see 1 Corinthians 12:10)
5. Effecting of miracles, or powers (see 1 Corinthians 12:10)
6. Eternal life (see Romans 6:23)
7. Evangelist (see Ephesians 4:11)
8. Exhortation (see Romans 12:8)
9. Faith (see 1 Corinthians 12:9)
10. Giving (see Romans 12:8)
11. Healings (see 1 Corinthians 12:9, 28)
12. Helps (see 1 Corinthians 12:28)
13. Interpretation of tongues (see 1 Corinthians 12:10)
14. Kinds of tongues (see 1 Corinthians 12:10; 1 Corinthians 14:1–34)
15. Leadership, or ruling (see Romans 12:8)
16. Mercy (see Romans 12:8)
17. Pastor, or shepherd (see Ephesians 4:11; Acts 20:28; 1 Peter 5:2)
18. Prophecy (see 1 Corinthians 12:10; 1 Corinthians 14:1)
19. Prophet (see 1 Corinthians 12:28; Ephesians 4:11)
20. Righteousness (see Romans 5:17)
21. Service (see Romans 12:7)
22. Teacher (see 1 Corinthians 12:28; Ephesians 4:11)
23. Teaching (see Romans 12:7)
24. Word of knowledge (see 1 Corinthians 12:8)
25. Word of wisdom (see 1 Corinthians 12:8)

Most of the above gifts are mentioned in four different places in the New Testament where we find gifts listed: Romans 12, 1 Corinthians 12, Ephesians 4, and 1 Peter 4.

Some people see other gifts within the pages of the Bible, such as craftsmanship, encouragement, fasting, hospitality, intercessory prayer, interpretation of dreams, judgment (being a wise judge), missions (cross-cultural ministry), music, philanthropy, and worship-leading. The scriptural support for such gifts has not been set forth in the form of a list, but it can be seen in biblical anecdotes and in various commands and directives.

Many Variations of Gifts

I believe that the gifts of the Spirit are as expansive as God Himself, so there is no reason to adhere rigidly to a particular set or listing of them as being exclusive or definitive. Even within the scriptural lists there can be variations of gifts, depending on their application. Take "teacher" or "teaching," for example. Some people teach adults, others teach children. Still others teach special groups only, such as the "differently abled" or international students. All teachers specialize in the topics they present to their students, and under any primary topic are large numbers of specialties. Music teachers, for instance, might teach how to play a particular instrument, the music of a particular culture, or how to lead worship music.

Additionally, most teachers prefer a particular method of delivery. A good number of teachers who call teaching their career express themselves verbally, to groups both large and small, many of them using technology to amplify and broadcast their voices. Other teachers do not actually verbalize much at all because most of their teaching is in written, published form. Some teachers are very informal, simply using the gift in the course of their daily communications with family members or business associates. Others employ a more formal style.

There are therefore many different kinds and methods of teaching. Would you consider each kind of teaching a separate gift or a subset of the main gift? Either way, we cannot put a limitation or boundary on the variety of gifts that God may give.

"Circumstantial Gifts," "Ministry Gifts," and "Office Gifts"

Some of the gifts of the Spirit seem to function in a temporary manner, according to the need of the moment. We might call these "circumstantial" gifts of the Holy Spirit. In other cases, believers operate consistently in one or more gifts; the gifts appear to reside within them. We can call these "ministry gifts" of the Holy Spirit. A select number of believers not only operate consistently in one or more gifts but have also been set apart as *gifts themselves* from God to the body of Christ to equip the church to do the works of Jesus. (See Ephesians 4:11.) This category of gifting is often referred to as the "offices," or "callings," of the Spirit.

THE SPIRIT IS READY TO RELEASE GOD'S GIFTS

The topic of the gifts of the Spirit is a marvelous one, and it is rather exciting to teach; but it is even greater to experience the gifts in action. Clearly, whether the gifting from God is circumstantial, consistent, or a calling for an extended period of time, it happens by the great grace of God alone. You cannot earn the gifts of the Holy Spirit. That is why they are called "gifts." And His gifts are still being released today!

Since the beginning of time, the Holy Spirit has desired to find people through whom He can manifest Himself, those who are open and receptive to Him. At creation, He "hovered" like a hen over her baby chicks before He created the world (see Genesis 1:2 NKJV, ESV, NIV), culminating in the making of human beings in God's image. More than two thousand years later, after the Exodus, Moses said, *"Would that all the Lord's people were prophets"* (Numbers 11:29). The prophet Joel foretold of a day when prophecy, dreams, and visions from God would become widespread. (See Joel 2:28–29.) After Jesus came to earth and the Spirit was given to the church, Peter announced that the day prophesied by Joel had arrived. (See Acts 2:14–18.) Again, we are still living in that day, and God is ministering His gifts to those who will receive them and release them for the benefit of the church and for the salvation of the world.

We must pray to be good stewards of the gifts of the Spirit as we seek three aspects of the Spirit's fullness in our lives: (1) fullness of power (the gifts of the Spirit), (2) fullness of character (the fruit of the Spirit; see Galatians 5:22–23), and (3) fullness of wisdom. Unless we have all three aspects of fullness, the gifts of the Spirit will be subject to misuse or disuse, and the kingdom of God will be long in coming. We must continue to grow and mature, conforming to the image of Christ, as we exercise spiritual gifts in godly character and wisdom.

Paul's words to Timothy apply to each one of us: *"Stir up the gift of God which is in you"* (2 Timothy 1:6 NKJV), and *"Do not neglect the spiritual gift within you"* (1 Timothy 4:14). Let's stir up our gifts, calling them forth for the glory of God. Come, Lord Jesus! Come, Father! Come, Holy Spirit! Fill us anew, right now!

⌣

Heavenly Father, I want to grow in all three dimensions of the Holy Spirit in my life. I ask for more of Your power, more of Your character, and more of Your wisdom ways. I ask You to be my Gift-giver, my Fruit-bearer, and my Teacher and Guide—always to Your glory. Without Your help, I cannot learn to live in a Christlike manner. As I walk through life, may I reflect Jesus by the power of the Holy Spirit wherever I go. Let me be continually open and receptive to the gifts You want to give me. I have great expectations that You will move in my life today! Amen and amen!

2

HOW THE HOLY SPIRIT MOVES

"'I will put My Spirit within you and you will come to life, and I will place you on your own land. Then you will know that I, the Lord, *have spoken and done it,' declares the* Lord*."*
—Ezekiel 37:14

The Holy Spirit loves messes. How do I know? Let's return to the second verse of the Bible: "*The earth was without form and void, and darkness was over the face of the deep. And the Spirit of God was hovering* ["*moving*" NASB] *over the face of the waters*" (Genesis 1:2 ESV). At creation, as the Holy Spirit was lingering over the formless nothingness, God spoke into being the world as we know it. The Spirit of God "loved" the chaos to life, transforming it from mess to magnificence.

Many Bible scholars apply "the law of first mention" to their study and interpretation of the Scripture; this principle maintains that the first time a word, a concept, or a doctrine is found in Scripture fixes its characteristics from that point forward. In the verse above, which is the second verse of the entire Bible, we see that the Spirit of God *moves*. And that is how He operates to this day. All the time, He keeps moving across the surface of the earth, and He brings light into darkness wherever He goes. He didn't stop moving that way after the earth was created, because He is constantly renewing the face of the earth, along with the hearts of the earth's inhabitants.

The most basic answer to the question "How does the Holy Spirit move?" is that He *hovers*. He stays over something until He chooses to move on, having completed His inspection or implementation. How should we respond to this information? Sometimes, our lives may feel like "formless nothingness," too, but the Holy Spirit within us is not inert. We can respond to His movements within us and around us today. We can open our hearts to receive the grace of God and to release it to others!

HOW TO RESPOND TO THE HOLY SPIRIT

I can think of at least three ways we should always respond to the Spirit. You and I should make it a point to...

1. Honor Him as a Guest—and Your Landlord

Welcome the Holy Spirit into your home, into your own spirit. Greet Him on a first-name basis, but without overfamiliarity. Acknowledge Him as the third person of the Godhead, with His own distinct personality and ways. As John the Beloved wrote, *"But when He, the Spirit of truth, comes, He will guide you into all the truth; for He will not speak on His own initiative, but whatever He hears, He will speak; and He will disclose to you what is to come"* (John 16:13).

Now, "guest" may not be the best word to use, actually. When we welcome the Spirit as a guest, we need to recognize Him not only as our Guest but as our Landlord. When we open the door for Him, He's not just making a guest appearance. Don't forget—He *owns* the place!

2. Seek His Presence

The Holy Spirit is more than our special Guest; He is also our Equipper. As we ask for Him, we must seek to be equipped by Him—continually—so that we can do the work of ministry. He is utterly generous with the gift of Himself, but He wants to be asked. Jesus put it this way:

So I say to you, ask, and it will be given to you; seek, and you will find; knock, and it will be opened to you. For everyone who asks, receives; and he who seeks, finds; and to him who knocks, it will be opened. Now suppose one of you fathers is asked by his son for a fish; he will not give him a snake instead of a fish, will he? Or if he is asked for an egg, he will not give him a scorpion, will he? If you then, being evil, know how to give good gifts to your children, how much more will your heavenly Father give the Holy Spirit to those who ask Him? (Luke 11:9–13)

If a son asks his father for a fish, he will not give him a snake, will he? Neither will the Holy Spirit give us a counterfeit or harmful gift. And He will never give us too little—or too much. We can never get too filled with Him, because He increases our capacity along the way, opening new rooms in our hearts, expanding us to receive more. Sometimes, in my journey with God, I feel as though He has almost done open-heart surgery on me. It is as if He has broken open my chest wall and exposed my heart so that He can come in more fully.

"Seek His presence" might sound a little mundane. Let me put it more animatedly: *Woo Him.* Create a magnetic atmosphere through worship that draws Him. Speak to Him words of blessing and wonder and celebration. Invite Him to be active in your life today.

3. Give Him Liberty to Take Charge

Once you have welcomed the Spirit into your innermost being, let Him take charge of you. When you allow Him to have full control, you will find true freedom. You will discover that the Spirit enables you to control the wrongful deeds of your fallen human nature.

Now the Lord is the Spirit, and where the Spirit of the Lord is, there is liberty. But we all, with unveiled face, beholding as in a mirror the glory of the Lord, are being transformed into the same image from glory to glory, just as from the Lord, the Spirit. (2 Corinthians 3:17–18)

The Spirit will change you—and you will like the results!

AVOID THESE NEGATIVE RESPONSES TO THE HOLY SPIRIT

Our ongoing relationship with the Holy Spirit is delicate. It can be damaged all too easily. For this reason, Scripture warns us against a number of attitudes and actions that can disrupt our bond with the Spirit.

1. Do Not Be Ignorant About the Spirit

Paul is big on this point. He reiterates it at least thirteen times in his epistles, writing, for example, *"Now concerning spiritual gifts, brethren, I do not want you to be ignorant"* (1 Corinthians 12:1 NKJV). Sad to say, much of the body of Christ *is* ignorant about spiritual gifts and the purposeful activity of the Holy Spirit. I'm not being judgmental when I state that simple fact. We need to educate each other about how to respond to the Spirit in our midst, teaching one another how to walk and live by the Spirit. (See Romans 8:4; Galatians 5:16, 25.)

2. Do Not Grieve the Spirit

Paul wrote much about how to cooperate with the Spirit of God. To the church in Ephesus, he said,

> Let no unwholesome word proceed from your mouth, but only such a word as is good for edification according to the need of the moment, so that it will give grace to those who hear. Do not grieve the Holy Spirit of God, by whom you were sealed for the day of redemption. Let all bitterness and wrath and anger and clamor and slander be put away from you, along with all malice. (Ephesians 4:29–31)

From this context, we understand that one of the most common ways we can grieve the Spirit is to treat our fellow human beings poorly. Negative, critical speech was as much a problem in Paul's day as it is in ours. And when we grieve the Spirit, He subsides. He's still there, but He steps back and waits for us to realize what we've done so that we can repent and repair the damage.

The Spirit won't grab us by the back of the collar and shake us until we cough out an apology. He will allow His seeming absence to weigh heavily on our spirits. We will miss Him, although sometimes it takes us a while to recognize that our fellowship with Him has been broken.

If we value the gentle presence of God's Spirit, we need to learn to replace our "unwholesome talk" with words of blessing and encouragement, and to curtail our negative thoughts and speech as soon as possible. You can do it right this minute, if you need to.

3. Do Not Insult the Presence of the Sensitive Dove of God

This warning is similar to the previous one. Not only is it possible to grieve the Holy Spirit, but it is equally possible to insult Him. When you insult someone, they shut down. They remove themselves from your presence as fast as possible, and they might not come back. There is a fair amount of emphasis in the church about the believer's need to be sensitive to the Dove of God, but something that also needs serious attention is the sensitive nature of the Dove Himself!

All four gospel writers report that when Jesus was baptized by His cousin John, the heavens opened and the Holy Spirit descended on the Son of God like a dove. (See Matthew 3:16; Mark 1:10; Luke 3:21–22; John 1:32.) This word picture is a meaningful choice. Doves are graceful and quiet. They are not self-centered, greedy, or pushy. And it doesn't take much to threaten them or to drive them away.

The author of the letter to the Hebrews addressed the matter of insulting the Holy Spirit by writing, *"How much severer punishment do you think he will deserve who has trampled under foot the Son of God, and has regarded as unclean the blood of the covenant by which he was sanctified, and has insulted the Spirit of grace?"* (Hebrews 10:29).

Let us always be reverent and respectful of the Spirit's sensitive nature.

4. Do Not Quench the Spirit

The apostle Paul gave the directive *"Do not quench the Spirit"* (1 Thessalonians 5:19). Or, as *Today's New International Version* translates it, *"Do not put out the Spirit's fire."* When you cover a flaming fire with a wet blanket, you quench it. Soon it smolders, then becomes cold ashes. People can quench the Spirit in many ways. Once again, treating others badly can quench the Spirit. How we treat each other is very important. Do we cultivate a culture of respect toward others? Do our leaders honor the people under their care, or do they merely tally them as numbers and try to control their behavior? Are husbands and wives treating each other with love and respect? Do they pay attention to scriptural directives for marriage, or do they think they are wiser than the Bible? There is much advice for us to follow throughout the New Testament about how to treat others with love and avoid quenching the Spirit.

5. Do Not Tempt, or Test, the Spirit

Another way of saying this would be, "Do not lie to the Holy Spirit." Dishonest Ananias and his wife, Sapphira, tempted the Spirit when they pretended that the amount of money they were donating to the church was the full amount they had received for a piece of property. (See Acts 5:1–11.) Each of them lied to Peter, who was the leading apostle of the church; but, in effect, they were lying to the Holy Spirit, because of course He knew the truth. Peter asked Sapphira, *"Why is it that you have agreed together to put the Spirit of the Lord to the test?"* (Acts 5:9). It would not have been wrong for them to have kept some or even all of the money, but it was sinful to make it look like they were more righteous and generous than they were.

It is a good thing that such lying does not always result in instant death, as in their case, or the church would be a much smaller institution than it is! Let us all consider the integrity of our words and our actions, whether we are interacting with people inside or outside of the church.

6. Do Not Blaspheme the Spirit of God

Blasphemy means cursing. We often hear God's name used *"in vain"* (Exodus 20:7) in the form of curses such as "Jesus" or "Christ" or "God." Certainly, such curses cannot be considered "wholesome speech" (see Ephesians 4:29), but they are forgivable. Not so for curses involving the Spirit. Here's what Jesus Himself said about it:

> *Therefore I say to you, any sin and blasphemy shall be forgiven people, but blasphemy against the Spirit shall not be forgiven. Whoever speaks a word against the Son of Man, it shall be forgiven him; but whoever*

speaks against the Holy Spirit, it shall not be forgiven him, either in this age or in the age to come. (Matthew 12:31–32)

This is intense. Make no mistake, it is one thing to quench or to offend the Holy Spirit, but it is an irreversible sin to utter a curse toward the divine Sustainer of Life, the Spirit of God. This is not what's at stake when someone speaks out of ignorance, for example, when someone attributes the works of the Holy Spirit to the devil. I am convinced that the seriousness of the offense against the Spirit depends on the degree of enlightenment a person has achieved. I can't believe that a person who has truly walked closely with the Holy Spirit would find it easy to repudiate Him or blaspheme against Him. (Note well that there are different interpretations of what constitutes blaspheming the Holy Spirit from what I have quickly presented here concerning this serious subject matter. But Jesus' warning from Matthew 12 shows how crucial it is for us to honor and reverence the Spirit and His work in our lives.)

HOW TO MOVE WITH THE SPIRIT

Okay, that is enough about how *not* to treat the Holy Spirit. Next, let's turn our attention to some constructive, scriptural advice about how any of us can learn to move with the Spirit successfully. As with everything else, scriptural exhortations are helpful foundations, but most of us learn best by observing the good examples of others in the body of Christ who have already discovered how to cooperate with the Holy Spirit. Do you know someone who exemplifies what it means to live and move with Him?

Walking with the Spirit means walking in the light of God. Some wise person once said that to move in the Holy Spirit means to flow with the Lord so closely as to not cast two shadows. I like that! Let's look now at what moving with the Spirit requires.

You Must Be Born of the Spirit

The idea of being *"born again"* (John 3:3, 7) comes directly from Jesus' discussion with the Pharisee Nicodemus. Before you can talk about learning to move with the Spirit, you must be born again. This does not happen by some formula or ritual but by a work of the Spirit. The Spirit is involved in our coming to faith initially, and when we hear His invitation, we must open the door of our hearts to Him and allow Him to give us spiritual new birth. In being *"born of the Spirit"* (John 3:6, 8), we give Him permission to do whatever He wants with our lives, and we ask Him to help us walk with Him.

You Must Receive and Be Baptized in the Spirit

There's no getting around this: if you wish to move with the Spirit, you must be baptized with the Spirit. You must allow yourself to be "immersed" in Him, allow Him to come upon you from the top of your head to the tips of your toes. Referring to Jesus, John the Baptist said, *"As for me, I baptize you with water for repentance, but He who is coming after me is mightier than I, and I am not fit to remove His sandals; He will baptize you with the Holy Spirit and fire"* (Matthew 3:11).

Like being born again, this experience does not come about through a particular formula or ritual; it is a work of the Spirit. You may or may not feel any "fire" of the Spirit when you are baptized by Him. Jesus' words to His followers before Pentecost apply to us today: *"You will receive power when the Holy Spirit has come upon you"* (Acts 1:8). The Spirit clothes us with Himself, and this happens when we receive Him and are baptized in Him. Jesus called the Spirit *"the promise of My Father"* (Luke 24:49). He wants us to receive the Father's promise, which is the gift of His own Spirit.

You Must Be Continuously Filled with the Spirit

As so many born-again, Spirit-baptized people have noticed, after we are filled with the Spirit, we tend to "leak" as we go through the circumstances of life. We lose track of the Holy Spirit. We grow dull. This does not mean that we need to be baptized in the Spirit over and over again, but we do need to be refilled repeatedly. In the original language of Paul's imperative *"be filled with the Spirit"* (Ephesians 5:18), the verb phrase *"be filled"* is a causative verb in the active voice. It literally means "go on being filled with the Spirit." A one-time filling will not last. Even if we did not "leak," we are still giving to others out of our overflow, and we need to continuously receive more of the Spirit in order to stay filled.

You Must Know the Spirit, Hear the Spirit, and See in the Spirit

Knowing the Spirit comes from hearing His whispers and following His voice. Knowing the Spirit enables us to see everything "in the Spirit"— through the Spirit's clear eyes. In exploring this reality, most of us have a long way to go, but we can eagerly seek to know Him better.

The first person of the Godhead that anyone meets is the Holy Spirit, because He's the One who convicts us concerning sin, righteousness, and the judgment to come. (See John 16:8.) The Holy Spirit is the One who knocks on the door of our hearts (see Revelation 3:20), and He is the One who makes Jesus a living reality to us.

The Spirit explains things to us. He speaks of new creation realities, and He shows us how to walk in the completed work of Jesus' cross. Jesus knew we would need the Spirit's help when He promised to send Him:

> *I will ask the Father, and He will give you another Helper, that He may be with you forever; that is the Spirit of truth, whom the world cannot receive, because it does not see Him or know Him, but you know Him because He abides with you and will be in you. I will not leave you as orphans; I will come to you.* (John 14:16–18)

We are no longer orphans once the Spirit of God has adopted us. We can embrace our new status as God's children with confidence. And, with practice, we can become so familiar with His voice that we will no longer turn a deaf ear (harden our hearts) when He speaks to us. (See, for example, Hebrews 3:15.)

The key for any operation of the gifts of the Holy Spirit is to know Him. It is important to know doctrine and spiritual principles, but it is more important to know the Holy Spirit Himself. With the gift of tongues, you can talk to God in the Spirit every day. (See chapter 10 of this book.) You can have a sustained personal relationship with the Holy Spirit. Do not harden your heart. Do not disobey what He has told you to do. Hear and obey—and live!

You Must Be Led by the Spirit as You Walk in the Spirit

You must be led by the Spirit because *"all who are being led by the Spirit of God, these are sons of God"* (Romans 8:14). People are supposed to be able to look at your life and tell that you are a child of God, as they see that you are being led by something other than your emotions, your logic, or even your renewed mind. You are being led by the Holy Spirit, the third person of the Trinity. You live in a different dimension from those who are not led by the Spirit.

The Holy Spirit comes alongside you to help in every circumstance, because He is your Helper. He's your Friend, your Comforter, the One who gives you strength and enables you to live according to the character and power of Jesus. *"So I say, walk by the Spirit, and you will not gratify the desires of the flesh* [sinful nature]*"* (Galatians 5:16 NIV).

The apostle John wrote that if we walk in God's light, the blood of Jesus cleanses us from all sin. (See 1 John 1:7.) It is important to note that the blood of Jesus cannot cleanse us if we are walking in the dark. If we persist in walking in darkness, we will become desensitized to the Spirit. But He will not challenge us; instead, He will wait for us and give us opportunities to turn back to Him so that we can walk free again.

You Must Pray in the Spirit

Paul wrote, *"I will pray with the spirit and I will pray with the mind also"* (1 Corinthians 14:15). We, too, need to pray both ways. By praying with our spirit in the Holy Spirit (that is, in an unknown tongue furnished by the Spirit), we can catapult beyond our natural understanding. As we will see when we come to chapters ten and eleven, the gift of tongues is not the least of the gifts of the Spirit, as many people assume. It is actually the entrance ramp into the other gifts. When you pray in the Spirit, you move into the realm of spiritual gifts; next, you might find the gift of faith, of wisdom, of a word of knowledge, of prophecy, of discerning of spirits, or of something else rising up. The apostle Jude summed up the importance of praying in the Spirit when he wrote, *"But you, beloved, build yourselves up on your most holy faith; pray in the Holy Spirit"* (Jude 1:20 NRSV).

HOW THE SPIRIT MOVES

It is not always easy to track with a Spirit who comes and goes like an invisible breeze. But we can depend on His promises to help us follow Him and learn His ways. It was the same for Jesus' disciples. For three years, they had walked closely with Him; and when He was about to be taken away from them to return to the Father, He reassured them that He would provide for them after He left, saying,

> *I tell you the truth, it is to your advantage that I go away; for if I do not go away, the Helper will not come to you; but if I go, I will send Him to you…. I have many more things to say to you, but you cannot bear them now. But when He, the Spirit of truth, comes, He will guide you into all the truth; for He will not speak on His own initiative, but whatever He hears, He will speak; and He will disclose to you what is to come. He will glorify Me, for He will take of Mine and will disclose it to you. All things that the Father has are Mine; therefore I said that He takes of Mine and will disclose it to you.*   (John 16:7, 12–15)

Jesus had a whole lot more to tell His disciples, and He was going to make sure that they could hear Him and follow Him, even though He was not physically present with them. Somehow the *"Spirit of truth"*—about whom the disciples knew very little—would come, and somehow He would *"guide"* them and *"disclose"* to them whatever they needed to know and understand.

As we now know, the coming of the Spirit happened on the day of Pentecost. (See Acts 2.) Immediately, the newly Spirit-baptized believers began to learn to identify the principles of how the Holy Spirit moves and acts. By paying attention, they could now move with Him and allow Him to work through them, wherever they were in the world. To this day, those of us who follow Jesus can do so only because His Holy Spirit is with us and in us.

Again, the Spirit reveals Jesus as a living reality and brings us into a deeper relationship with Him in an ongoing way. Jesus introduces us to the Father, just as He said: *"I am the way, and the truth, and the life; no one comes to the Father but through Me"* (John 14:6). And as Jesus reveals the Father, the

Holy Spirit reveals Jesus. It is an interdependent cycle, and we are privileged to participate in it. The Holy Spirit reveals the unified counsel of God the Father and God the Son. The Spirit doesn't talk about Himself; He talks about the Father and Jesus. He listens to Their conversations, and He speaks about what He hears, on *Their* initiative, not independently on His own.

The Spirit always knows exactly what God wants to do in our lives. That is why praying in the Spirit is so effective. As Paul wrote,

> *In the same way the Spirit also helps our weakness; for we do not know how to pray as we should, but the Spirit Himself intercedes for us with groanings too deep for words; and He who searches the hearts knows what the mind of the Spirit is, because He intercedes for the saints according to the will of God.* (Romans 8:26–27)

The Holy Spirit is our life-giving Source, the One who brings us into the life of the Lord Jesus. He makes true disciples of us, because He is interested in maturing our character more than in bringing us personal comfort. He brings us truth, not false assurance or false comfort. He convicts, persuades, shepherds, and leads us to the life-source of God. He helps us to overcome our fears, and He stretches us beyond ourselves, moving us to testify of the love and power of God and showing us how to bear fruit that lasts. (See John 15:16.)

We can get to know the Holy Spirit because He lives inside us. We can lean into Him, walk with Him, live with Him, listen to Him. We can depend on Him to always lead us out of darkness and into the light.

Additionally, we must keep in mind that, in all that He does, the Holy Spirit never moves contrary to the written Word of God. He complements it and does not compete with its instructions and doctrines. We would do well to store up the words of Scripture so that we will have a functioning plumb line in our own spirits. That way, when we think the Spirit is telling us something, we can see if it is in alignment with the Word. We can verify our visions and dreams or adjust our understanding of them. We can catch ourselves early on when we start to walk in an unbalanced way. We can activate our spiritual gifts confidently and capably. And we can enjoy the journey!

OPEN YOURSELF TO THE SPIRIT

How does opening ourselves to the Holy Spirit work in real life? How can we prepare and position our spirits so that we can move with God's Spirit?

Initially, we must learn the value of quieting ourselves. We need to stop hurrying so much. When our spirits and minds are like stirred-up fishbowls or shaken-up snow globes, we can't hear what He's saying. The psalmist knew this secret: *"I wait for the LORD, my soul does wait, and in His word do I hope. My soul waits for the Lord more than the watchmen for the morning; indeed, more than the watchmen for the morning"* (Psalm 130:5–6).

These days, we sometimes call the process of waiting in the presence of the Lord "soaking." This is when you get your spirit's tank refilled with the Holy Spirit, and it is best to establish a pattern of doing it the first thing in the morning so that you can return to that inner place of peace and trust anytime throughout the day, finding your satisfaction in Him. The psalmist compared a quieted soul to a contented young child who has been well cared for, whose hunger has been fully satisfied: *"My soul is like a weaned child within me"* (Psalm 131:2).

Once we have quieted ourselves, we can seek out God. Throughout the day, we can exercise the gift of tongues; we can pray in the Spirit. This builds our faith very effectively and turns us toward the Father's heart. Paul wrote to the Corinthians, *"I speak in tongues more than you all"* (1 Corinthians 14:18), and what he meant was that he relied heavily on this gift, to the point that he may have used it more than all of the Corinthians put together.

Earlier in my ministry, the Holy Spirit indicated to me that if I would pray in the Spirit for two hours before I was scheduled to address God's people, He would give me a spirit of revelation. I really wanted that, but I didn't see how I could devote two hours straight to praying in tongues. So, I got a stopwatch, and I broke the time down into fifteen-minute increments throughout the day. Then the Spirit corrected me: *I didn't say two hours in a day. I said two hours in one sitting.* I obeyed, but I had to build my spiritual muscles in order to do it. I decided to sing in the Spirit, and when I did that, I got lost in prayer and worship. The two hours didn't seem long anymore; and, true enough, the spirit of revelation started increasing in my life. It was a wonderful preparation for flowing in the Spirit.

An important part of opening ourselves to the Holy Spirit is making a conscious determination to be a participant in whatever He wants to do, instead of remaining merely a passive observer. When you go to worship meetings, you should be ready to get involved, eager to give and not only to receive. At the minimum, you should be an intercessor, praying for those who are leading the meeting, "holding up their arms" as Aaron and Hur held up Moses' arms in order to bring victory to the Israelites. (See Exodus 17:8–13.) Stir up your faith and believe that God wants to use "little ole me," as Randy Clark says, to impart His love to others.

Even if you are having a proverbial "bad day," you can still allow God to use you. On your worst day, you've got something alive within you that you can give away. It is the hope of glory. True hope is something the world just does not have. When you are walking and moving in the strength and counsel that the Spirit supplies, you are operating in God's grace.

Ask the Holy Spirit for a fresh revelation of His grace. You already know that you cannot earn the gifts of the Spirit or access the power of God without grace. When you move with the Spirit in God's grace, all the credit and all the glory returns to God, where it belongs.

Gracious Father, in You I live and breathe and have my very being. I am totally dependent upon You. I rejoice that You are so accessible and that the gifts of Your Spirit come to me by grace and not by my own performance. I pause to say, "Thank You! I love You and Your ways!" Now I ask You to move upon my life in fresh encounters with Your Holy Spirit, who is my Helper, my Guide, and my personal Tutor. Come, Holy Spirit; I want to receive You and release Your presence and Your gifts everywhere I go. I am excited about the new adventures I am embarking upon with You! I praise You, Lord! Amen!

3

HOW TO GROW IN EXERCISING SPIRITUAL GIFTS

"Pursue love, yet desire earnestly spiritual gifts…. Since you are zealous of spiritual gifts, seek to abound for the edification of the church."
—1 Corinthians 14:1, 12

When Jesus told His disciples, *"I will not leave you as orphans"* (John 14:18), He was also speaking to us—to anyone who hears His words and believes in Him. If Jesus had not fulfilled this promise, enabling us to be adopted into the heavenly family of His Father God, you and I would be orphans, having no spiritual position and being unable to provide for ourselves. But He did follow through, and we have been adopted as God's sons and daughters. Jesus welcomed us into His family by giving us gifts, each one of which keeps on giving within the context of the family. His spiritual gifts have been set solely within the framework of a fellowship of believers—the body of Christ. *"For by one Spirit we were all baptized into one body,…and we were all made to drink of one Spirit"* (1 Corinthians 12:13).

God shines His brilliant light through the gifts. He illuminates our innermost beings (see Proverbs 20:27), and He shows His glory to the world at large. Jesus said, *"You are the light of the world. A city set on a hill cannot be hidden; nor does anyone light a lamp and put it under a basket, but on the lampstand, and it gives light to all who are in the house"* (Matthew 5:14–15).

In other words—even as much as independent-minded Americans might resist the idea—the spiritual gifts are not given to isolated individuals because, by definition, anybody who has been adopted into the family of God is no longer alone. We are not orphans, and none of us is an only child. Spiritual gifts are given only within a community setting, and they shine forth with collective brightness. Remember, the new wine is found in the cluster. (See Isaiah 65:8.)

A CULTURE OF HONOR, LOVE, AND SERVANTHOOD

Therefore, where spiritual gifts are concerned, you are not an independent agent. Did you know that? You cannot exercise your spiritual gifts in isolation, apart from other people. We need each other's ministry. We need each other's encouragement in the faith. And we flourish within a culture where believers are *"devoted to one another in brotherly love; [giving] preference to one another in honor"* (Romans 12:10).

Just as the worldwide body of Christ functions like a human body, so does every local assembly of believers, with each member having a specific function. The entire body is necessary. (See 1 Corinthians 12:12–31.) We find safety and accountability there, and in truth our gifts cannot work as they were intended outside of the body. What good is a nose or an eye all by itself?

Exercising our spiritual gifts is not a competition; it is a collaboration, and each one of us needs to take a humble position, even as we work with all of our energy. Our identities and pride should not be caught up in our giftedness; we should recognize the fact that we are only one part of a larger body. Let's review the passage in Romans 12 where Paul talks about spiritual gifts:

> *For just as we have many members in one body and all the members do not have the same function, so we, who are many, are one body in Christ, and individually members one of another. Since we have gifts that differ according to the grace given to us, each of us is to exercise them accordingly: if prophecy, according to the proportion of his faith; if service, in his serving; or he who teaches, in his teaching; or he who exhorts, in his exhortation; he who gives, with liberality; he who leads, with diligence; he who shows mercy, with cheerfulness.* (Romans 12:4–8)

In a healthy fellowship, we all serve each other. Nobody claims a seat of honor. The apostle is willing to set up chairs, and the prophet cheerfully sweeps the floor when necessary, because each person finds his or her identity in Christ. We must defer to one other and give others opportunities to exercise their gifts. (See, for example, 1 Corinthians 14:26–32; Hebrews 5:14.)

I remember being with my friend Ché Ahn, the apostolic founder of the network of churches called Harvest International Ministry (HIM), based in Pasadena, California. We were ministering at a church in Alabama at a leaders' meeting before a public conference began. I had a relationship with the church, and I was helping to introduce Ché Ahn and HIM for possible apostolic affiliation. We had a nice meal together and shared our hearts with one another. Then Ché got up and started clearing off the tables. He was simply being himself, performing an act of kindness. The leaders' hearts were won over that night. By what? The great vision? The amazing testimonies from around the world? Possibly. But I believe that what really convinced that group of leaders to say yes to the invitation to partner with HIM was Ché Ahn's spirit of servanthood. Gifts flourish in an atmosphere of servanthood.

EXERCISING SPIRITUAL GIFTS IS ACTIVE, NOT PASSIVE

As I wrote earlier, you must stir up the gifts within you. You can't just go sit in a worship service and hope that the Spirit will move you in some way. You need to take some action. Remember that Jesus told us to *go:*

And He said to [His disciples], "Go into all the world and preach the gospel to all creation.... These signs will accompany those who have believed: in My name they will cast out demons, they will speak with new tongues; they will pick up serpents, and if they drink any deadly poison, it will not hurt them; they will lay hands on the sick, and they will recover."... And they went out and preached everywhere, while the Lord worked with them, and confirmed the word by the signs that fol-lowed.   (Mark 16:15, 17–18, 20)

God waits for His people to go forth so that He might demonstrate the power of the cross of Christ and impart life to the spiritually hungry. Signs follow believers who move out into the world with the gospel. Signs confirm the truth—for believers and nonbelievers alike. The crucial initial step is for believers to move. There is no "sit" in the Great Commission; it is "Go"!

Never let a sort of religious perfectionism make you passive. Take risks. Spend yourself. Get up and go do something. If you hesitate because you do not feel ready, and you keep on waiting until you have collected "more"—more confidence, more strength, more wisdom, more experience, more power, and so forth—you will never start to give to others out of your giftedness. But if you will do something with the little bit that you have, God will multiply your little "loaves and fishes." When you act generously out of what you have already, doing as the Spirit indicates, you will be sur-prised at how much more will be multiplied back to you. Exercising your spiritual muscles always makes them stronger.

You will learn to exercise your spiritual gifts with maturity only if you use them. As I emphasized in the preface to this book, practice makes per-fect. The more you practice, the more proficient you will be. Again, just give from what you have received from your Father, and expect—even ask outright—to receive more. Your Father stands ready to give you more graces and gifts from His Spirit. (See, for example, Matthew 7:11; Mark 11:24.) *"This is the confidence which we have before Him, that, if we ask any-thing according to His will, He hears us. And if we know that He hears us in whatever we ask, we know that we have the requests which we have asked from Him"* (1 John 5:14–15).

How can you be fully confident that you are asking for the right thing? Because of the work of God's Spirit in your heart. The New Testament keeps telling us to ask and receive because, as we earnestly seek God, He changes the desires of our hearts to match His. As we delight ourselves in the Lord, our requests line up with His will, and we end up asking for exactly what He knew we would need. (See Psalm 37:4.) That is really the way it works! As former orphans, we can rejoice in the new life God has given us. *"For all who are being led by the Spirit of God, these are sons of God"* (Romans 8:14).

Bear in mind that certain gifts are always within the will of God to ask for in prayer, such as the gifts of prophecy, tongues, and interpretation of tongues. (See 1 Corinthians 14:1, 5, 13.) In other words, you can never go wrong by asking for these gifts. Do step out and do *something*. Just move out in faith today, stirring up your gift and asking God for more—all for the sake of the people around you: *"So also you, since you are zealous of spiritual gifts, seek to abound for the edification of the church"* (1 Corinthians 14:12). Double-check your motives. Never let your exercise of a gift become a performance, especially if your gift puts you on the platform in front of others. Remember, you are not building your own little kingdom. Rather, you have been adopted into God's family, making you a citizen of *His* kingdom!

SOWING AND REAPING

The saying is true—what you sow, you will reap. (See 2 Corinthians 9:6.) You may ask me, "James, what does that have to do with receiving and exercising spiritual gifts?" Well, *everything!* Let me tell you some personal stories to illustrate.

When I was much younger, I sowed into the ministry and life of Mahesh Chavda of All Nations Church in Charlotte, South Carolina. Some people might call what I did being an "armor-bearer." I carried his bags, interceded for him, brought him coffee or a hot drink when he was praying for the sick for hours on end, and served in similar ways. One time, when we were in Prague, Czech Republic, I went back to the hotel room to retrieve his tennis shoes because his feet were getting tired from standing and praying over hundreds of people, one by one. At times, on my own time and with my own money, I helped to set up his meetings in the Midwest and New England. I did up-front work for a crusade in Haiti. It was my delight to serve this humble man of prayer and fasting who moves in extraordinary signs and wonders to this day.

Well, guess what happened? You sow and then you reap. I sowed into the life of this healing evangelist, and what did I reap? A bona fide miracle: the healing of my sweet wife from medically documented barrenness. We could not have children—not even close. But Mahesh, under a prophetic anointing, declared that we would have children, even though it was humanly impossible. And, four miracles later, we knew the principle of sowing and reaping!

Here is one more example that will encourage your heart. Ché Ahn, whom I mentioned earlier as the founding apostle of Harvest Ministries International, was hosting a number of conferences in different parts of the United States and in other countries. As an apostle, he befriended some well-known prophets, such as Lou Engle, Jill Austin, Stacey Campbell, and me. Ché was not as gifted in a revelatory way then as he is today. But I know why he changed. After having invited these prophets into his life, he received a *"prophet's reward"* (Matthew 10:41). What was the reward? An increase in the spirit of revelation in his own life.

You reap what and where you sow! Therefore, if you want to grow in receiving and releasing spiritual gifts, then serve in a certain sphere and see what the Lord will do. The more you give away, the more you will receive. The more you sow into another person's life and ministry, the more you will grow. It is the way the kingdom of God operates!

VARIETIES OF GIFTS, MINISTRIES, AND OPERATIONS

As mentioned earlier, there is almost infinite variety in the ways in which the Spirit of God expresses Himself through spiritual gifts, ministries, and various operations or actions. Paul greatly expanded our understanding of this reality when he wrote, *"Now there are varieties of gifts, but the same Spirit; and there are varieties of service* ["*ministries*" NASB], *but the same Lord*" (1 Corinthians 12:4–5 ESV). He concluded this idea by saying, "*There are varieties of activities, but it is the same God who empowers them all in everyone*" (2 Corinthians 12:6 ESV). Ministries are made up of a collection of gifts; and the wide variety of gifts, expressed through different personalities, is further varied by the surrounding circumstances.

As much as we might like to achieve cookie-cutter uniformity in the expression of the gifts (an inclination that comes from insecurity and a desire for control, it seems to me), we can't get away from the fact that the Holy Spirit expresses Himself with endless creativity. There is just no single, "right" way to implement the gifts (although, for the sake of order, it is helpful to follow certain protocols). Accordingly, in one place of ministry, people will line up at the front to receive prayer for healing. In other places, you will find healing rooms and "soaking" prayer. Elsewhere, a simple declaration of "Be healed!" will be effective. Some churches will promote a five-stage healing model, while others will not have a clue what that healing model is. At times, it is a matter of environment. Some people's gifts do not seem to be very well developed when they are at their home church, but as soon as they get out among the general population, their gift of prophetic evangelism, for one example, really shines.

We can learn from each other without imitating every detail. Although you may be impressed to see how the Spirit worked in a particular situation with another gifted believer, you do not need to follow suit step-by-step—unless the Holy Spirit leads you to do so. Each person should follow the Spirit's lead in each situation. For example, just because you saw someone blow on the microphone when they prayed for the Spirit to come into a room doesn't mean that you need to do it, too. Let the Spirit do things His way! We are not called to be copycats. We are called to be secure in our identity in Christ and to release the unique expression of His gifts in our lives to the people around us. And to enjoy the whole creative journey!

Despite the great variety of expression, everything stems from the same God, doesn't it? The same Holy Spirit has inspired believing men and women across cultures and class distinctions throughout the centuries, right up to this present minute. He expresses His grace in a distinct manner each time He is allowed to work in and through somebody. He does not limit Himself to working through "religious professionals" or even to a particular polished mode of expression. Our Creator is utterly creative, and His life flows through any member of His body who will open the floodgates of their heart to Him.

The all-important thing is love. In 1 Corinthians 12:31, Paul wrote, *"But earnestly desire the greater gifts. And I show you a still more excellent way."* Next, he went on, in his famous Love Chapter, 1 Corinthians 13, to extol the supremacy of love. He closed out his discussion of the relationship between spiritual gifts and love by mentioning the importance of pursuing love *along with* the spiritual gifts: *"Pursue love, yet desire earnestly spiritual gifts"* (1 Corinthians 14:1).

Love attracts love. God's Holy Spirit is on the move, and He is looking for people who belong to Him. *"The eyes of the LORD move to and fro throughout the earth that He may strongly support those whose heart is completely His"* (2 Chronicles 16:9). I want be found and supported by Him, don't you?

BUILD YOUR FAITH

If we're going to step out of our comfort zone and use or release our spiritual gifts, most of us need ongoing encouragement. Where can we find the best words of encouragement? In the Word itself! The New Testament is rich with faith-building words about spiritual gifts, and we will explore them in depth in the remaining chapters of this book. Build your own faith by praying, by reading straight through the following Scriptures and other selected verses, and then by rising up and declaring them as true for you. Stir up your own Spirit-given gift mix.

> *To each one is given the manifestation of the Spirit for the common good.... But one and the same Spirit works all these things, distributing to each one individually just as He wills.* (1 Corinthians 12:7, 11)

> *As each one has received a special gift, employ it in serving one another as good stewards of the manifold grace of God. Whoever speaks, is to do so as one who is speaking the utterances of God; whoever serves is*

to do so as one who is serving by the strength which God supplies; so that in all things God may be glorified through Jesus Christ, to whom belongs the glory and dominion forever and ever. Amen.

(1 Peter 4:10–11)

If you then, being evil, know how to give good gifts to your children, how much more will your heavenly Father give the Holy Spirit to those who ask Him? (Luke 11:13; see also Matthew 7:11)

Do not be deceived, my beloved brethren. Every good thing given and every perfect gift is from above, coming down from the Father of lights. (James 1:16–17)

Pursue love, yet desire earnestly spiritual gifts, but especially that you may prophesy.... Now I wish that you all spoke in tongues, but even more that you would prophesy.... Since you are zealous of spiritual gifts, seek to abound for the edification of the church.... Brethren, do not be children in your thinking; yet in evil be infants, but in your thinking be mature.... When you assemble, each one has a psalm, has a teaching, has a revelation, has a tongue, has an interpretation. Let all things be done for edification. (1 Corinthians 14:1, 5, 12, 20, 26)

And it shall come to pass in the last days, says God, that I will pour out of My Spirit on all flesh; your sons and your daughters shall prophesy, your young men shall see visions, your old men shall dream dreams. And on My menservants and on My maidservants I will pour out My Spirit in those days; and they shall prophesy.

(Acts 2:17–18 NKJV, quoting Joel 2:28–29)

You will receive power when the Holy Spirit has come upon you.

(Acts 1:8)

In everything you were enriched in Him, in all speech and all knowledge, even as the testimony concerning Christ was confirmed in you, so that you are not lacking in any gift, awaiting eagerly the revelation of our Lord Jesus Christ. (1 Corinthians 1:5–7)

And my God will supply all your needs according to His riches in glory in Christ Jesus. (Philippians 4:19)

The outpouring of the Holy Spirit on Pentecost is one of the greatest things that ever happened, on top of the incarnation and the resurrection of the Lord Jesus Christ. Since then, the Holy Spirit has been moving throughout the earth, patrolling the territory and winning hearts. The influence of the outpoured Spirit outstrips all of the apparent increase in Satan's wicked power that we see in these latter days. (See, for example, 1 Timothy 4:1; 2 Timothy 3:1–5, 13.) We live in fearful times. But by overcoming our fears with faith, we can be part of God's plan to overtake evil and win once and for all.

SIGNS WILL FOLLOW

God ordained that the gospel should be preached with signs following. (See what happened in the early church, for example, in Mark 16:15–20; Acts 8:5–7; 28:1–10; Romans 15:18–19; Hebrews 2:3–4.) There are more "heathen" in the world today who have not heard the gospel than there were in the days of the apostles! Therefore, in our lifetimes, we can expect to see the darkness overcome by unprecedented, brilliant displays of God's grace and supernatural power—through His gifted people, as we preach the salvation message of Jesus Christ.

I started this chapter with the good news that we do not have to scramble to live a good life in our human strength. Jesus has not abandoned us to an earth-sized orphanage. Instead, through Him, we have been adopted into His Father's heavenly family, and He is now our eldest Brother. Within the bosom of God's family, we find everything we need concerning *"life and godliness"* (2 Peter 1:3)—and that includes giftedness. We can rest completely on this promise: *"My God will supply all your needs according to His riches in glory in Christ Jesus"* (Philippians 4:19).

Turn around for a moment and take a look. Are signs and wonders following you? Do you see behind you a string of testimonies about the gifts of the Holy Spirit—not just from yesterday, but also from today? Is your faith active? Are you casting a shadow of Jesus by standing in the light of

God's love, His Word, and His deeds? How "dangerous" are you, anyway? As for me, I want to see signs following! Do I hear an amen? Amen!

⌒

Father, in the great name of Jesus, I declare that I am receiving more of the precious Holy Spirit, and I am committed to activating and releasing the gifts You give to me. I choose to create a culture of honor toward the Word of God and toward the messengers of God who are in my life today. I believe that what I sow, I will reap. I therefore stir myself up in the Holy Spirit, and I expect rivers of living water to flow out of me everywhere I go. I am expecting radical things to happen! In Jesus' mighty name, amen.

SECTION TWO

REVELATORY GIFTS—THE GIFTS THAT REVEAL

In this section, I begin an examination of each of the nine gifts. For ease of presentation and description, I group the gifts together in three different sets of three gifts each. The first set is the gifts that reveal, the second set is the gifts that do, and the third set is the gifts that speak.

We begin our study of the gifts that reveal in chapter 4 with a look at the gift of discerning of spirits. This gift provides perception into the spirit world, which includes the Holy Spirit, both good and evil angelic spirits, and individual human spirits. You will see that the gift of discernment can be cultivated. Accordingly, your senses can be trained so that, over time, you can learn from experience how to interpret what your senses pick up.

In chapter 5, we survey the gift of a word of wisdom. This gift enables people to speak clearly and compellingly about God's all-wise purposes, conveying His loving guidance to whole governments as well as to individuals. I make it clear that you do not have to be advanced in age or schooled in theology to operate in this gift, because it is a gift from the Spirit, not a product of your intellect. The gift of a word of wisdom can come to us in a variety of ways, such as an internal "nudge," a "quickened" Scripture, an angelic visitation, a vision, or a dream.

In chapter 6, we focus on the gift of a word of knowledge. I use this point in the book to explain, by means of the example of a rainbow, that the nine gifts are not as separate and distinct as we might imagine. The borders that define them can be blurred, just as the individual colors of the rainbow blend with the colors next to them. Very often, you cannot discern where one gift ends and another one begins. Still, each of the gifts retains its own distinctive hue.

In this chapter, I explain that a word of knowledge usually comes to us by a quiet impression or sense. We could call this "hearing internally," or having a "gut feeling." You just "know that you know," but not how you know it. There is no way that any human being—even the smartest person the world has ever seen—can know everything. But God does. He is omniscient, knowing all things, even the deepest secrets. And through the gift of a word of knowledge, He shares parts of His knowledge with His sons and daughters. We might say that a word of knowledge relates to information, while a word of wisdom relates to instruction. I also note that the gift of a word of knowledge overlaps with gifts of healings and workings of miracles, helping to create an atmosphere of faith.

4

THE GIFT OF DISCERNING OF SPIRITS

"Beloved, do not believe every spirit,
but test the spirits to see whether they are from God."
—1 John 4:1

When I was growing up, some of the kids were still playing cowboys and Indians, but most of us had moved on to war games and outer-space adventures. The Cold War had settled in after World War II, which meant that nukes and ray guns were part of every red-blooded American boy's arsenal of imaginary weapons. And if we needed to detect enemy contamination, a discarded shoebox and a toilet paper tube could be assembled into a fully functional Geiger counter. The click-click-click of the Geiger counter could indicate how much "radiation" was in our backyard.

DEFINING THE GIFT OF DISCERNING OF SPIRITS

The gift of discerning of spirits (*"distinguishing of spirits"* in some translations; see 1 Corinthians 12:10 NASB, NIV) operates a bit like a spiritual Geiger counter in detecting a source that is not apparent to the natural senses but nevertheless is present and is exerting some form of influence. The gift provides perception into the spirit world—which includes the Holy Spirit, both good and evil angelic spirits, and individual human spirits. It gives supernatural insight into the realm of spirits.[1]

It can sometimes be hard to tell where supernatural activity originates, because not all of it comes from the Holy Spirit. Only someone who can penetrate more deeply with spiritual eyes can tell the difference between supernatural activity from the Holy Spirit and from elsewhere.

> The gift of discerning of spirits is the God-given ability or enablement to recognize the identity (and very often the personality and condition) of the spirits which are behind different manifestations or activities....
>
> The dividing line between a human and divine operation may be obscure to some believers, but one with the faculty of spiritual discernment sees a clear separation.[2]

Individuals who are gifted with this supernatural gift of perception can perceive "the motivating spirit behind certain words or deeds."[3] Sam Storms, Bible teacher and former visiting associate professor of theology at Wheaton College, suggests that the gift of discerning of spirits is "a supernaturally enabled sense or feeling concerning the nature and source of [a] spirit." He proposes that "this spiritual gift may be the ability to pass discerning judgment on prophetic utterances, thereby standing in relation to the gift of prophecy the way interpretation does to the gift of tongues."[4]

To discern means to distinguish, to differentiate, or to perceive, and people exercise the gift of discernment in different ways, often through their senses. Some receive the revelation visually, some "just know," and some hear or taste perceptively, while others have a heightened capacity to feel differences and discernments.

We each must surrender our five natural senses to the Holy Spirit and practice discerning good from evil. (See Hebrews 5:14.) In God's kingdom, we can learn to be "naturally supernatural" and "supernaturally natural." But there is always a big learning curve. No one starts out being able to discern perfectly. I have been at this for forty-plus years, and I am still discovering fresh ways to move in the gifts of the Holy Spirit, including the gift of discerning of spirits.

SPECIALTIES OF DISCERNMENT

As with any of the gifts, this gift is expressed in specific ways through different people. Some people have an anointing to distinguish spirits in the angelic realm. Further, their anointing may single out one of their five senses. I know a person who can discern angels readily but who does not see anything in the demonic realm. Other people may use the gift of discerning of spirits largely in intercessory warfare prayer, where it helps them to distinguish territorial spirits of darkness over a region. Others might be specially gifted in ministering personal deliverance; such people are able to discern whether a person's own spirit is simply in distress or if a demonic spirit, such as a "religious spirit," is causing conflict and turmoil. People who have a pastoral bent will be able to apply their discernment to the human spirits of others in order to help them figure out the mixture of motivations within them. I happen to have a lot of dreams when I'm sleeping, and I need to be able to discern their significance. Sometimes, an angel may appear in a dream in a symbolic capacity, and the dream carries a message that I need to decipher; but other times an actual angel visits the room, and the first thing I notice when I wake up is that the atmosphere is powerfully permeated with heavenly purpose.

Whether or not the person is a "seer" who can see what the Spirit is doing, someone with the gift of discernment of spirits can *perceive* what's going on. Perception occurs in many different ways. I have a friend who feels a kind of weight on his shoulders, recognizes it as supernatural, and can figure out what it means each time. Others feel something like fire resting on top of their heads. If you have this gift, you will learn by experience how to interpret the signals. It is great to have so many kinds of special discernment within the body of Christ, and we need every kind of godly discernment we can get!

In my life and ministry, I have found that the gift of discerning of spirits functions well in public ministry settings as well as in private settings for intercessory purposes. For example, I had a stretch of time a few years back when I would "see" flames of fire resting over individuals in the audience for whom the Spirit was about to do something glorious. All I had to do was to announce His presence. I would hear a *whoosh* and see a flame of fire over the head of someone in the audience. Then I would point to the person and say, "All right, this person over here in the third row..." and the flame would go down inside the person, and he or she would "go down" into the Spirit's glory realm, sometimes falling out of his or her seat. God did wonderful things for people, including physical healing, and I didn't have to do anything else after pointing out that the Spirit was about to work.

Prophetic seer Bob Jones taught me so much about the discernment of spirits. In the late 1980s and 1990s, we were a part of the birth of the modern-day prophetic movement in Kansas City. Almost daily, Bob saw angels, engaged in spiritual warfare with demons, and discerned the very presence of the Holy Spirit Himself. I learned how to submit my five natural senses to the Holy Spirit's anointing from this unusual forerunner.

In recent years, I have had many opportunities to partner with my dear friend Cindy Jacobs of Generals International, watching her move swiftly from the natural realm into the supernatural, perceiving realm—sensing angels, detecting demonic presence, or manifesting the awesome holiness of God. I believe this is her highest gifting, and she shows me new possibilities every time we minister together!

NEW TESTAMENT GLIMPSES OF DISCERNMENT

We see different categories of discernment illustrated throughout the New Testament accounts of Jesus' ministry and that of the early church.

Discerning the Holy Spirit

John the Baptist discerned the Holy Spirit when the Spirit descended upon Jesus from heaven like a dove at His baptism. (See, for example, Matthew 3:13–17.) John didn't let familiarity get in the way of discernment. Remember, Jesus was John's cousin, and they were about the same age. They probably knew each other well, and perhaps even played together as children. And yet, John may not have been sure that Jesus was the Messiah until he saw the dove. (See John 1:32–34.) About three years later, the believers in the upper room on the day of Pentecost discerned the presence of the Holy Spirit as the sound of rushing wind and then as tongues of fire resting on their heads. (See Acts 2:2–3.) We do not know if they could discern these things with their natural ears and eyes or if it was entirely supernatural; but in any case, they agreed on what they had experienced.

Discerning Angels

Scripture says that an angel appeared to Jesus in the garden of Gethsemane, *"strengthening Him"* (Luke 22:43). After Jesus' resurrection, Mary saw two angels in the sepulcher where Jesus' body had been laid. (See John 20:11–13.) An angel appeared to Paul to give him a message of reassurance when he was in the midst of a violent storm at sea. (See Acts 27:23–24.) Angels do not look or act the same at all times; therefore, it takes divine discernment to know whether or not what you are seeing is actually an angel that you can trust.

Discerning Human Spirits

From afar, Jesus discerned a guileless spirit in Nathanael. (See John 1:47–48.) Shortly thereafter, He discerned the opposite of a guileless spirit in people who believed in Him only for His miracles. (See John 2:23–25.) Years later, Peter famously discerned the wrong motives of Simon the magician:

> Peter said to him, "May your silver perish with you, because you thought you could obtain the gift of God with money! You have no part or portion in this matter, for your heart is not right before God. Therefore repent of this wickedness of yours, and pray the Lord that, if possible, the intention of your heart may be forgiven you. For I see that you are in the gall of bitterness and in the bondage of iniquity." But

Simon answered and said, "Pray to the Lord for me yourselves, so that nothing of what you have said may come upon me." (Acts 8:20–24)

On the positive side again, Paul discerned a "spirit of faith" in a lame man in Lystra:

At Lystra a man was sitting who had no strength in his feet, lame from his mother's womb, who had never walked. This man was listening to Paul as he spoke, who, when he had fixed his gaze on him and had seen that he had faith to be made well, said with a loud voice, "Stand upright on your feet." And he leaped up and began to walk. (Acts 14:8–10)

You would not expect to find any faith in a man who had been lame since birth. He had never walked in his life! Yet he carried hope that if he waited long enough, something good would happen. After looking at him intently, Paul could discern the man's faith, and he proceeded to simply tell the man to walk. He didn't do that with every lame beggar he passed. But Paul was well-attuned to the Spirit so that when he came to this particular beggar, he paused and took time to discern what the Spirit wanted to do.

Discerning Evil Spirits

During His earthly ministry, Jesus discerned many evil spirits manifested in various forms. Once, He cast out a spirit of infirmity that was causing a woman to have serious curvature of the spine. This deliverance from an evil spirit resulted in the woman's immediate healing, yet Jesus didn't make the incident into a spectacle. In fact, He did not address the unclean spirit at all:

There was a woman who for eighteen years had had a sickness caused by a spirit; and she was bent double, and could not straighten up at all. When Jesus saw her, He called her over and said to her, "Woman, you are freed from your sickness." And He laid His hands on her; and immediately she was made erect again and began glorifying God.
(Luke 13:11–13)

Jesus laid His hands on the woman, and without any additional words, the evil spirit departed, as demonstrated by her immediate ability to stand up straight. I call this "leaning in"—making an evil spirit leave simply by bringing the Spirit of God too close for the evil spirit's comfort. Often, when I discern an unclean spirit and want to get rid of it, I can also discern when I do not need to speak to the spirit. By leaning in, I'm counting on the reality that the Spirit of God dwells in me, and that *"greater is He who is in you than he who is in the world"* (1 John 4:4).

The apostles also discerned evil spirits. When Paul and Silas were preaching in Philippi, a businesswoman named Lydia believed and came to the Lord. But then a slave girl trailed Paul and Silas around the city, bothering them by persistently announcing to the public, by means of a spirit of divination, who they were. Her interruptions were not helping their preaching, because apparently, every time she made a pronouncement, it was as if a nullifying blanket of unbelief was cast over the place. Finally Paul had had enough, and, without warning, he dispatched the evil spirit: *"Paul was greatly annoyed, and turned and said to the spirit, 'I command you in the name of Jesus Christ to come out of her!' And it came out at that very moment"* (Acts 16:18). Nobody had to tell Paul, "This slave girl is prophesying by the power of an unclean spirit." He was simply able to discern it. After he cast out the evil spirit with the commanding word, the atmosphere was cleansed. Now their preaching could break through. It seems that this turn of events agitated Satan. The girl's masters incited the people and the public officials against Paul and Silas so that they were arrested and put in prison. But before long, revival broke out in that prison, with the jailor and his whole family receiving Christ.

A quite different New Testament example of discerning of spirits occurs in the great revelational vision of the apostle John, in which he noted that he saw three unclean spirits that looked like frogs. (See Revelation 16:13.) Frogs were likely considered unclean by the Israelites since the plague of frogs at the time of the exodus from Egypt, and they were specifically declared unclean by God with the giving of the law. (See Leviticus 11:9–12.) Today, we can sometimes discern the presence of evil spirits by seeing a vision of a particular evil-seeming animal in association with a person or a situation.

These are only a handful of the many notable occasions when the gift of discerning of spirits came into play in the New Testament. I am sure that, many times, the gift was operating in "undercover" ways, just as it does today, without being mentioned at all. Unless this gift is in operation, the church cannot achieve—and maintain—health and growth.

PURPOSES OF THE GIFT OF DISCERNING OF SPIRITS

Obviously, one of the primary purposes of the gift of discerning of spirits is for the sake of people's *deliverance*. This is what we see when Jesus encountered the Gerasene demoniac. (See Mark 5:1–20.) Jesus arrived in the region, discerned and cast out the *"legion"* of demons in the man, and then went away. He didn't stick around to preach or to work miracles. Deliverance of that one man was the entire purpose of Jesus' visit to the area of the Gerasenes.

A related purpose of the gift of discerning of spirits is to reveal and expose the servants of Satan and to put a halt to their work and utterances. This is what happened when Paul exposed the evil motives of Elymas the magician: *"Saul, who was also known as Paul, filled with the Holy Spirit, fixed his gaze on him, and said, 'You who are full of all deceit and fraud, you son of the devil, you enemy of all righteousness, will you not cease to make crooked the straight ways of the Lord?'"* (Acts 13:9–10). And later, in Philippi, after Paul had discerned and cast out the evil spirit from the slave girl, not only did evangelism take root in the region, but the slave girl's owners could no longer exploit her demonic gift for financial gain.

Additionally, the gift of discerning of spirits is a vital help in exposing false prophets and satanic error in doctrine. We read in Paul's first letter to Timothy, *"The Spirit explicitly says that in later times some will fall away from the faith, paying attention to deceitful spirits and doctrines of demons, by means of the hypocrisy of liars seared in their own conscience as with a branding iron"* (1 Timothy 4:1–2). John provided a useful test for verifying discernment in this regard; you could call it the "Jesus is Lord" test. If a person's spirit has been captured by an antichrist spirit, that person cannot confess Jesus' lordship:

Beloved, do not believe every spirit, but test the spirits to see whether they are from God, because many false prophets have gone out into the world. By this you know the Spirit of God: every spirit that confesses that Jesus Christ has come in the flesh is from God; and every spirit that does not confess Jesus is not from God; this is the spirit of the antichrist, of which you have heard that it is coming, and now it is already in the world.... We are from God; he who knows God listens to us; he who is not from God does not listen to us. By this we know the spirit of truth and the spirit of error. (1 John 4:1–3, 6)

Anyone can apply this test. A fallen angel or demonic spirit simply does not have the ability to state the truth that Jesus Christ has come in the flesh as the Son of God. I have applied this scriptural test in many different situations, and it works in any cultural setting. Be sure to add this important assessment tool to your personal discernment kit.

As you can see, the underlying purpose of the gift of discerning of spirits is so that a person can follow the moving of the Holy Spirit. By the operation of this gift, a person can better cooperate with the Spirit, whose movements are often so discreet as to be almost imperceptible. The Scriptures describe the Holy Spirit as being like the wind: *"The wind blows where it wishes and you hear the sound of it, but do not know where it comes from and where it is going; so is everyone who is born of the Spirit"* (John 3:8; see also Ezekiel 37:9–10).

John Wimber was unusually gifted in the ability to discern the Holy Spirit's movements in corporate settings. I remember being in meetings with him where he would announce, "He is coming like the sea across the ground right now. A light is starting over here, and it is moving across people in this direction." And the glory of God would spread over the people like an oncoming wave.

GUIDELINES FOR OPERATING IN THE GIFT OF DISCERNING OF SPIRITS

The only way to learn your own "language" for the gift of discerning of spirits is through practice; the gift can be cultivated. Your senses can be trained, and over time you can learn from experience how to interpret what your senses pick up. Scripture says, *"Solid food is for the mature, who because of practice have their senses trained to discern good and evil"* (Hebrews 5:14). You can also immerse yourself in the Word so that you can recall key truths, as needed, to confirm your senses. This will also keep certain scriptural advice in the forefront of your mind, such as the idea of examining the spirits with the "Jesus is Lord" test.

Sometimes, the clearest way to understand your discernment is to examine the fruit of a person's life. Is it good fruit or not-so-good fruit? Jesus said,

> *You will know them by their fruits. Grapes are not gathered from thorn bushes nor figs from thistles, are they? So every good tree bears good fruit, but the bad tree bears bad fruit. A good tree cannot produce bad fruit, nor can a bad tree produce good fruit. Every tree that does not bear good fruit is cut down and thrown into the fire. So then, you will know them by their fruits.* (Matthew 7:16–20)

Keep an eye on the fruit within your own life, too. The gift of discerning of spirits is not the "gift of suspicion." Your insights and perceptions should never be used in gossip or for purposes of defamation, but always for edification and building up the body of Christ. The Holy Spirit wants to cure and mend the members of the body, not harm them. Never ally yourself with the accuser of the brethren, the devil! (See Revelation 12:10.)

As you can see, the gift of discerning of spirits has the potential to be explosive; therefore, it is crucial to use wisdom while exercising it. To keep from learning everything the hard way (and potentially doing damage), obtain wisdom beyond your years by consulting others who have greater experience with the gift. In addition, stir up companion gifts, such as faith.

I have noticed that revelatory gifts such as this one can be accompanied by extra faith to act or to pray with authority. Get into the habit of praying a discernment or a revelation back to the Father before you act on it. Seek His guidance for the application of what you have received. At the least, you can always intercede in prayer. Spirit-guided intercession is always appropriate. But if He seems to indicate it, you may release a command to rebuke an enemy you have discerned.

God will guide you all along the way; just keep up an ongoing conversation with Him. With the apostle Peter, I say to you, *"Grace and peace be multiplied to you in the knowledge of God and of Jesus our Lord; seeing that His divine power has granted to us everything pertaining to life and godliness"* (2 Peter 1:2–3).

ARE YOU HUNGRY FOR MORE?

Are you satisfied with your own level of discernment, or do you believe the Lord has more for you? Even writing this chapter has caused a fresh hunger for discernment to rise up within me. I want to more precisely perceive the operational spiritual forces that are behind things; and when they are forces of darkness, I want to displace them and release more of the brilliant light of God's kingdom rule and reign. That is why I believe that we should *ask* for this gift of the Holy Spirit. *"You do not have because you do not ask"* (James 4:2; see also John 16:24). Are you going to be passive and say that the gift of discerning of spirits is for apostles and prophets only? I hope not! Let me emphasize again that these gifts are not toys for us to play with on public platforms; they are tools for building God's kingdom. He is waiting for us to become all we can be in Christ Jesus. Come on! Step up to the plate with me!

⌒

Dear Lord, I am not satisfied! I want more of Your Spirit's presence, power, and gifting. In Jesus' great name, I ask right now for an increase of the gift of discerning of spirits. I want to be able to know the very moving of the Holy Spirit, to detect angels, to displace demons, and to discern the inner motivations of the hearts of men and women. I ask for an increase. Move on my five natural senses and give me lessons and practice. Thank You for the increase! In Jesus' mighty name, amen.

5

THE GIFT OF A WORD
OF WISDOM

*"Yet among the mature we do impart wisdom, although it is not
a wisdom of this age or of the rulers of this age.... Now we have
received not the spirit of the world, but the Spirit who is from God,
that we might understand the things freely given us by God. And we
impart this in words not taught by human wisdom but taught by the
Spirit, interpreting spiritual truths to those who are spiritual."*
—1 Corinthians 2:6, 12–13 (ESV)

When I was just fourteen years old, I picked up a special prayer burden for God's wisdom, and I am still carrying it. My Sunday school teachers had taught me about Joseph and Daniel and Esther and Nehemiah and others from the Bible who were like them— people who exhibited remarkable wisdom. This caused me to start to pray consistently for three things: (1) for wisdom beyond my years, (2) for God to raise up "Joseph counselors" for those in authority, and (3) for a pure heart. So, even before I really knew what these things meant, I was praying for a spirit of wisdom, a spirit of counsel, and a heart of purity.

For years now, I have prayed that God would raise up Solomons as well as Josephs—for people of authority who possess God's wisdom for their jurisdictions, and also for wise counselors for people who are in authority. I know that, with wise insight and counsel, 9/11-type disasters can be averted. Enemies can be captured. Wars can be ended. God's wisdom covers everything, on both an individual and a global level.

Decades later, I am still praying for a spirit of wisdom. In fact, I believe I need it more now than I did when I was a youth. I have gained a good amount of wisdom, often by hard-knocks experience and what I would call "lessons from the woodshed," and I have seen answers to that prayer in my life, especially as I have navigated my way through various church movements: evangelical, charismatic, Jesus People, Word of Faith, discipleship, third wave, prophetic, apostolic reformation—and probably more that I have left out. As I have experienced difficult wisdom lessons along the way, I have learned to pray for wisdom for my fellow travelers on the journey, as well. With the apostle Paul, "*I keep asking that the God of our Lord Jesus Christ, the glorious Father, may give you the Spirit of wisdom and revelation, so that you may know him better*" (Ephesians 1:17 NIV).

I remember one time when I heard the Holy Spirit whisper to me a word of wisdom that was more like a paragraph of wisdom: *Lack of communication breeds misunderstanding. Misunderstanding can lead to accusation. And accusation unattended to always leads to some form of alienation.* That was a true word of wisdom, and I have drawn on that revelatory insight many times in tight situations. The gift of a word of wisdom is enormously needed to help bring what I call "hope solutions" into people's lives and into churches, cities, and nations!

Although the gift of a word of wisdom is one of the most needed gifts, it may be one of the most overlooked in the body of Christ. We are overrun with prophetic revelation and factual knowledge, but we often lack the wisdom to know what to do with them! As Derek Prince said,

"Knowledge gives us facts and wisdom shows us what to do about those facts."[1] Without the help of the Holy Spirit, we cannot interpret and apply revelations appropriately.

DEFINING THE GIFT OF A WORD OF WISDOM

I love Sam Storms's definition of the gift of a word of wisdom. He suggests that it may be "the ability to articulate life-changing insights into God's mysterious, saving purposes for mankind, both on a global plane as well as in application to individuals."[2] The reason I appreciate this particular slant on the gift is that it emphasizes the *giving* aspect more than the *receiving* aspect. The gift of a word of wisdom enables people to speak clearly and compellingly about God's all-wise purposes, conveying His loving guidance to whole governments (as Joseph did in Egypt) as well as to individuals within the church.

Do you have to be advanced in age before you can exercise a gift of wisdom? Not at all; Joseph and Solomon were in the prime of their lives. Must you attain a theological degree or achieve a certain status within the body of Christ? No, it is bestowed supernaturally as the Holy Spirit decides.

Dick Iverson, founding pastor of City Bible Church (Oregon), formerly called Portland Bible Temple, says, "It is not 'a' word of wisdom but 'the' word of wisdom. It is not just a word on the subject or the situation at hand, it is 'the word' [God's own word] on it." It is a word that expresses "the will of God in that situation."[3] John Wimber noted that it reveals part of the total wisdom of God for the immediate situation, and that it does not depend on human logic. He called it "transrational," which includes the rational but goes above and beyond it.[4] God's wisdom is totally transrational: "'For My thoughts are not your thoughts, nor are your ways My ways,' declares the LORD" (Isaiah 55:8).

The gift of a word of wisdom is a vital adjunct to both the gift of a word of knowledge and the gift of prophecy. For example, when prophets are predicting times of upheaval and desperation, we need God's wise spokespeople to help us understand what to do. The church needs to provide

God's solutions, not just diagnose the problems (which the world already spends most of its time doing). We are supposed to be solution people, not problem people.

On a personal level, you need God's wisdom to carry you through all of the ups and downs of your daily life. You also need the spirit of wisdom to help you know what to do when you receive a prophetic word or impression. Are you supposed to just intercede about it? Or are you supposed to speak it? If so, to whom? In what way? How long should you "sit on it"?

The fact is, you can never have too much wisdom!

WISDOM THAT RESOLVES CONFLICTS

Scripture abounds with examples of the gift of wisdom in action. Let's look with fresh eyes at one of the most famous displays of true wisdom—Solomon's decision about a dispute over a baby. (See 1 Kings 3:16–28.) Previously, Solomon had asked God to give him wisdom and knowledge to rule the Israelites well, which God granted him. (See 2 Chronicles 1:8–12.) Now, he was presented with a real challenge in arbitrating this dispute. Two women (harlots, actually) who shared a house had just given birth to baby boys within a day of each other. One had rolled over in her sleep one night and accidently suffocated her son. When she made the horrifying discovery in the middle of the night, she got up and stealthily switched her dead baby for the live one who was sleeping next to his mother. She was determined to have a live son.

The second woman was the one who brought the case to Solomon for a decision. I'm sure passions were high in front of the judgment seat.

The one woman said, "…When I rose in the morning to nurse my son, behold, he was dead; but when I looked at him carefully in the morning, behold, he was not my son, whom I had borne." Then the other woman said, "No! For the living one is my son, and the dead one is your son." But the first woman said, "No! For the dead one is your son, and the living one is my son." Thus they spoke before the king.… The king said, "Get me a sword." So they brought a sword before the king. The king said, "Divide the living child in two, and give half to the one and half to the other." Then the woman whose child was the living one spoke to the king, for she was deeply stirred over her son and said, "Oh, my lord, give her the living child, and by no means kill him." But the other said, "He shall be neither mine nor yours; divide him!" Then the king said, "Give the first woman the living child, and by no means kill him. She is his mother." When all Israel heard of the judgment which the king had handed down, they feared the king, for they saw that the wisdom of God was in him to administer justice.

(1 Kings 3:17, 21–22, 24–28)

When Solomon said, "*Get me a sword,*" did that sound like a word of wisdom? Possibly even Solomon didn't quite know what he was going to do next, if God had not yet told him what to do with the sword. "*Get me a sword*" was not a logical thing to say; it was definitely transrational! But when he proposed slicing the infant into two equal pieces, he flushed out the true mother, because she cared more that the little boy not be killed than about her claims as his mother. The deceitful mother's hard-hearted response confirmed Solomon's decision. The word of wisdom he gave solved an unsolvable conflict and caused all of the people to respect him for it. Justice prevailed.

This conflict-resolving gift is just as important today as it was in the past, and God is still offering His wisdom to those who seek Him.

WISDOM THAT CONFOUNDS DECEPTION

You are probably familiar with the incident in the New Testament in which the Pharisees were trying to trip Jesus up, so they asked Him whether or not it was lawful to pay the hated poll tax to Caesar. They thought they had Him this time, because they knew there could be no perfect answer to the question. Jesus perceived (discerned[5]) that they intended to trap Him, and He gave the following cagey response:

"Why are you testing Me, you hypocrites? Show Me the coin used for the poll-tax." And they brought Him a denarius. And He said to them, "Whose likeness and inscription is this?" They said to Him, "Caesar's." Then He said to them, "Then render to Caesar the things that are

Caesar's; and to God the things that are God's." And hearing this, they were amazed, and leaving Him, they went away.

(Matthew 22:18–22)

Jesus did not meet the Pharisees on their level; He met them with wisdom they did not know existed, wisdom from a superior plane, and He threw them off successfully, leaving them puzzling as to how He did it.

WISDOM THAT SOLVES PROBLEMS

After Jesus ascended to heaven, the brand-new church relied on the gift of a word of wisdom again and again. Nobody had ever done what they were doing; there was no precedent for them to follow. So, they did the best thing they could do—they relied on the Spirit for direction.

That's how the role of deacons was "invented." The church leaders were getting stretched too thin as the apostles had to divide their time between preaching and running a "soup kitchen" for needy widows—and there were further demands because the believers from non-Jewish backgrounds felt that their widows were being shortchanged. Scripture does not say, "The apostles started looking for strong volunteers who had the gift of helps/service." Instead, undoubtedly guided by wisdom from on high, they advised the people to look for men who had the gift of *wisdom* who could take care of the distribution of food to the widows:

*So the twelve summoned the congregation of the disciples and said, "It is not desirable for us to neglect the word of God in order to serve tables. Therefore, brethren, select from among you seven men of good reputation, **full of the Spirit and of wisdom**, whom we may put in charge of this task.*

(Acts 6:2–3)

I find it fascinating that they specifically wanted high-caliber men of wisdom to perform practical tasks. And they found the men they needed: *"They chose Stephen, a man full of faith and of the Holy Spirit, and Philip, Prochorus, Nicanor, Timon, Parmenas and Nicolas, a proselyte from Antioch"* (Acts 6:5).

HOW TO RECEIVE AND RELEASE A WORD OF WISDOM

As I wrote earlier, when I was a young man, I traveled with Mahesh Chavda as an assistant. One day, I asked him, "Mahesh, I see so many miracles happen in your ministry. What is your key to hearing the voice of the Spirit?" I wanted to learn his secret. He told me something simple—but not easy: "You must understand, the closer I get to Him, the gentler His voice becomes."

In other words, he often "heard" the Spirit's voice as no more than a divine impression, perceived in his heart through spiritual intuition, like a quiet "nudge." This is the way the early apostles were led, too, as we can see in the following instances from the life of Paul:

> They [Paul and those who were traveling with him] *passed through the Phrygian and Galatian region, having been forbidden by the Holy Spirit to speak the word in Asia; and after they came to Mysia, they were trying to go into Bithynia, and the Spirit of Jesus did not permit them.*   (Acts 16:6–7)

> *And now, behold, bound by the Spirit, I am on my way to Jerusalem, not knowing what will happen to me there....*   (Acts 20:22)

In the first passage, look at how Paul and his coworkers expressed themselves. They were hindered, turned away from their intended course of action, "*forbidden by the Holy Spirit*," not permitted to enter Bithynia. In the second Scripture, Paul was "*bound by the Spirit*" on his way to persecution in Jerusalem. The Spirit did not say, "Thou shalt not!" from the midst of a thundercloud. His guiding hand was not obvious, but they had learned to be as sensitive to His subtle pressures as well-trained, obedient horses are to the slight tugs and pulls of their masters' reins.

We see also that they did not shy away from receiving warnings. In fact, we learn from these passages that the gift of a word of wisdom often serves as an early warning system for those who are walking closely with the Spirit.

I have received redirection in this way more than once. In each case, finding myself unsettled about some aspect of my plans, I consulted the Spirit. He revealed just enough to help me change my plans appropriately. Perhaps I was going to walk into a trap or a compromising situation. Thanks to the Spirit, I felt hindered from following through on my plans. My conscience was disquieted until I changed my plans, and then it was at peace.

Many times, wisdom will come to us in a little more direct manner—some word or line of Scripture speaks directly to our situation; it comes alive, as if God were speaking directly to us (which He is). This is called a "quickened" word from the Lord. An example of this is when Peter advised the early church about replacing Judas. He quoted a couple of psalms that applied to the situation at hand. (See Acts 1:15–26.) Later, after Peter had brought some Gentiles to the faith, which distressed the members of the church who were staunchly Jewish, James quoted the prophet Amos to defend him. Luke recorded how he rendered a wise decision based on that word of Scripture:

> After they had stopped speaking, James answered, saying, "Brethren, listen to me. Simeon has related how God first concerned Himself about taking from among the Gentiles a people for His name. With this the words of the Prophets agree, just as it is written, 'After these things I will return, and I will rebuild the tabernacle of David which has fallen, and I will rebuild its ruins, and I will restore it, so that the rest of mankind may seek the Lord, and all the Gentiles who are called by My name,' says the Lord, who makes these things known from long ago. Therefore it is my judgment that we do not trouble those who are turning to God from among the Gentiles."
>
> (Acts 15:13–19, quoting Amos 9:11–12)

Of course, internal nudges and scriptural guidance are not the only ways the Holy Spirit shares God's will with His people. Sometimes, He sends an angel, as He did when Paul was on board the storm-lashed ship that looked like it was going to sink, an incident we looked at briefly in the previous chapter. Paul told the crew,

Men, you ought to have followed my advice and not to have set sail from Crete and incurred this damage and loss. Yet now I urge you to keep up your courage, for there will be no loss of life among you, but only of the ship. For this very night an angel of the God to whom I belong and whom I serve stood before me, saying, "Do not be afraid, Paul; you must stand before Caesar; and behold, God has granted you all those who are sailing with you." (Acts 27:21–24)

In a similar way, God sometimes sends a word of wisdom by means of a vision or a dream (which is a vision received during sleep). This is how the Spirit reassured Paul when he was working in Corinth: *"The Lord said to Paul in the night by a vision, 'Do not be afraid any longer, but go on speaking and do not be silent; for I am with you, and no man will attack you in order to harm you, for I have many people in this city'"* (Acts 18:9–10).

Also remember another scriptural example—the time the Spirit directed Peter to go to the home of the devout Roman centurion Cornelius through a vision that Peter received while in a trance. (See Acts 10:1–23.)

Wisdom is not the same as prediction, although without a doubt, God knows what is going to happen. When He sends us His wisdom for a situation, He is helping to direct our steps. He wants us to cooperate with Him for the sake of spreading His kingdom on earth; this cooperation can span every category of human involvement, from personal health decisions to international war alliances. This is why the gift of a word of wisdom can sometimes only be exercised corporately, such as when leaders discuss and work together to arrive at a decision by consensus. They take counsel together, which is good, because *"in a multitude of counselors there is safety"* (Proverbs 24:6 NKJV; see also Proverbs 11:14 NKJV). This keeps headstrong individuals from taking off in the wrong direction and dragging other people with them. We see this method of wisdom-seeking in the accounts of the early church, as *"the apostles and the elders met together to consider this matter"* (Acts 15:6 NRSV). (See also Acts 6:1–7; 15:1–31; 21:15–25.)

So we see that wisdom often concerns future events and developments, but it does not foretell them as much as it supplies insights, revelations, commands, and instructions that arise out of God's knowledge of those upcoming circumstances.

THE WAY, THE TRUTH, AND THE LIFE

Jesus is *"the way, and the truth, and the life"* (John 14:6). His life is a demonstration of the way of wisdom. The Spirit of this God-Man now lives in every Christian; Jesus has been made for us the wisdom of God (see 1 Corinthians 1:30 KJV), and *"we have the mind of Christ"* (1 Corinthians 2:16).

Again, this inner impartation of wisdom can solve individual, church, and national problems. Any complex situation can be untangled by the spirit of wisdom. True wisdom shows the way. It produces conviction, open hearts, open doors, unanimity, progress, justice, and whatever else is needed in challenging times.

To tap into God's vast supply of wisdom, all you have to do is just wait in quietness. Worship, trust, assimilate. Get saturated with the spirit of revelation and wisdom. Immerse yourself in the wisdom of the written Word and take advantage of any opportunity to sit at the feet of those who are wiser than you.

When any one of us asks for wisdom from above, we should expect to receive it. (See James 1:5–8.) This spirit of wisdom is available to us all through Christ, in keeping with Isaiah 11:1–4. Additionally, those who have been given the consistent gift of a word of wisdom will be able to cultivate an ongoing supernatural flow of divine understanding that can greatly benefit the body of Christ and the world at large. Along those lines, right now in my own study and contemplation, I am praying to understand a related subject that I am calling "divine intelligence." Daniel walked in it, and I am convinced that God wants to put this level of divine insight into many people's lives through His Spirit of wisdom. Today, leaders such as Ed Silvoso and Lance Wallnau and many others are pioneering fresh applications for this gift, such as societal transformation. Out of God's inexhaustible supply, which is not at all tied up or out of reach, we can ask for and receive wisdom from above and release it to those who need it, for the rest of our lives.

You can apply Paul's prayer for the Ephesians to yourself and to anyone you pray for:

I keep asking that the God of our Lord Jesus Christ, the glorious Father, may give you the Spirit of wisdom and revelation, so that you may know him better. I pray that the eyes of your heart may be enlightened in order that you may know the hope to which he has called you, the riches of his glorious inheritance in his holy people, and his incomparably great power for us who believe. (Ephesians 1:17–19 NIV)

Holy Father, I boldly ask for the spirit of wisdom and revelation to operate in my life. I need an increase of the gift of a word of wisdom to be able to solve complex problems with a simple word. Grant me Your divine intelligence. Give me the mind of Christ as I welcome the release of Your wisdom into my life and ministry, for Jesus Christ's sake. Again, I say, amen.

6

THE GIFT OF A WORD
OF KNOWLEDGE

*"My goal is that they may be encouraged in heart and united in love,
so that they may have the full riches of complete understanding, in
order that they may know the mystery of God, namely, Christ, in
whom are hidden all the treasures of wisdom and knowledge."*
—Colossians 2:2–3 (NIV)

Suppose you just stepped out your door into the sunshine after a big rainstorm. Wow—look at that gorgeous rainbow against the dark sky! It is the biggest and brightest one you have ever seen. You whip out your smart phone and record a short video to share with your family and friends. Later, you start looking at it on the screen. You never really studied an actual rainbow before. You realize that it doesn't have clear lines of demarcation between the colors. You can see red-orange-yellow-green-blue-indigo-violet, and the spectrum is beautiful, but the boundaries of the colors blur together; new colors were created and shifted in tone even as you panned from one side to the other.

You thought you were just taking a video of a rainbow, but you were doing more than that; you were recording a delightful analogy of the gifts of the Spirit, which blend together like the colors of the rainbow. Very often, you cannot discern where one gift ends and another one begins. It's a good thing, too! This blending is exactly what we need. For example, a gift of discerning of spirits can enable someone to single out an unclean spirit, but you or somebody else must have the gift of faith in order to cast it out. And the gift of wisdom, which you just finished reading about in the previous chapter, so often overlaps and blends with the revelational gift of knowledge that it can be difficult indeed to distinguish a dividing line between them.

God's Spirit supplies His people with gifts as needed, although most of us do not recognize the wealth of resources we have to work with. His power is not limited by artificial definitions, including our interpretations of His written Word. His range is so much broader and bigger and brighter and more beautiful than any "spectrum analyzer" can reveal.

Still, each of the gifts in God's rainbow retains its own distinctive hue. Now let's explore the gift of a word of knowledge to find out what it looks like.

DEFINING THE GIFT OF A WORD OF KNOWLEDGE

No way could any human being—even the smartest person the world has ever seen—know everything. But God does. He is omniscient, knowing all things, even the deepest secrets. And through the gift of a word of knowledge, He shares parts of His knowledge with His sons and daughters. So we can say that a word of knowledge "pertains to *information*" (as compared to a word of wisdom, which "pertains to instruction").[1]

The church has understood this gift in at least two distinct ways, illustrated by the following quote from apostolic teacher Peter Wagner:

The gift of knowledge is the special ability that God gives to certain members of the Body of Christ to discover, accumulate, analyze and clarify information and ideas that are pertinent to the growth and well-being of the Body....

Note: Pentecostals and charismatics often use the term "word of knowledge," which is information that God gives by revelation for a certain situation [including details about a person's life]. My interpretation of the charismatic "word of knowledge" is that such a gift is in reality a subset of the gift of prophecy, not the gift of knowledge. A scholar, on the other hand, would be one who has a gift of knowledge.[2]

The above fits well with the rainbow analogy. Yet regardless of what kind of knowledge we mean, the fact that the word of knowledge is a spiritual gift signals the fact that this knowledge is supernaturally derived. It "does not come by natural reasoning, education, or training but directly by the Holy Spirit."[3] For example, a person's willpower will never to be able to catch hold of a word of knowledge to speak it; each word can be delivered only at God's sovereign determination.

In this chapter, I prefer to follow the Pentecostal/charismatic/third wave approach to the gift of a word of knowledge. Looking at it this way, the word of knowledge is the gift that is used to "call out" someone for further ministry in a meeting in which the spiritual gifts are active. The revelation of details about a person that could not otherwise be known by the speaker, such as the person's name, physical circumstances, and hidden needs, provides convincing proof that God wants to bless that person beyond his or her limited expectations. Such a word is "an utterance inspired by God and spoken by an individual. It is an insight into the things freely given us by God. It shares the truth the Spirit wishes to be declared concerning a specific occasion, person, or thing."[4] It is "the supernatural revelation of facts about a person or situation, which is not learned through the efforts of the natural mind, but is a fragment of knowledge freely given by God, disclosing the truth which the Spirit wishes to be made known concerning a particular person or situation."[5]

CREATING AN ATMOSPHERE OF FAITH

The gift of a word of knowledge has a lot to do with the culture of the supernatural in a church setting, and it overlaps into the gifts of healings and workings of miracles, helping to create an atmosphere of faith. It is not necessarily that a word of knowledge heals but that it releases confidence to people that God knows the details of their situation and that He loves them. Faith rises up, and the atmosphere becomes pregnant with expectancy; people feel that almost anything can happen.

Not that every word of knowledge culminates in a healing or a miracle. Sometimes, people do not respond. Perhaps more information is needed, or perhaps fear tamps down faith. Or—as in the case below—sometimes we don't see the healing or the miracle because the person responds secretly, without telling anyone.

I was ministering in Bangkok, Thailand, and I had seen a remarkable fulfillment of prophecy the previous day after receiving a word of knowledge for a woman in the audience. But this day was quite different. Here's how I told the story in the first chapter of the book *Adventures in the Prophetic*:

> The whole atmosphere of the place was charged with expectation. These people had watched the other prophecy and now they thought I could call anybody out by name, birth date, and Social Security number.... [But this time,] I didn't have much to go on.
>
> In fact, only one thing kept cycling around in my mind. Finally I spoke it out: "There is a seventeen-year-old boy, a son of someone here, and he is backslidden and on drugs. He is going to give himself to the Lord tonight."
>
> Nothing happened. Everybody was looking at me but nobody was responding [I went back to preaching, but the insistent word made me stop twice more in hopes that someone would respond]....
>
> After the close of the meeting, I was supposed to leave the auditorium and go back to my hotel to bed because I had to teach again the next day. But somehow I could not leave. That same word was *still* cycling around and around in my tired head. Finally, almost

everybody had left. A young janitor came into the auditorium to put the chairs away. I got into a conversation with him, because he spoke English.

Turns out he was seventeen years old. And he was on drugs. And he was a backslider. And he had actually rededicated his life to Jesus that night. He had been there, hanging around the back of the auditorium and listening to the meeting, and he had realized that word was for him. He just didn't say so in public.[6]

PURPOSES OF THE GIFT OF A WORD OF KNOWLEDGE

Producing Conviction

In the above case, the word of knowledge penetrated the heart of the young janitor in Thailand and brought him to conviction and conversion. In a similar way, when Jesus met the Samaritan woman at the well, He confronted her with a word of knowledge that brought her—and many of her neighbors—to the point of conviction. Knowing already that she did not have a husband, Jesus said to her, "*'Go, call your husband and come back.'* *'I have no husband,' she replied*" (John 4:16–17 NIV). Then Jesus detailed His word of knowledge: "*You are right when you say you have no husband. The fact is, you have had five husbands, and the man you now have is not your husband. What you have just said is quite true*" (John 4:17–18 NIV).

Before long, "*many of the Samaritans from that town believed in him because of the woman's testimony, 'He told me everything I ever did.' So when the Samaritans came to him, they urged him to stay with them, and he stayed two days*" (John 4:39–40 NIV). In actual fact, Jesus had not told her "everything" she had ever done, had He? But this shows the supernatural power of a revelation such as this, because by revealing only a small sliver of truth about her life, the word convinced and convicted the sinful woman. She knew for a fact that she was in touch with the God who knows all things, and she wanted to surrender herself to Him. (For the full account, see John 4:4–40.)

Preparing People for a Future Event

Besides conviction, another purpose of a word of knowledge is preparation—to help get someone ready for a future event. This seems to happen more often as we walk in increasing closeness with the Lord. For example, toward the end of his life, Paul said, *"And now, compelled by the Spirit, I am going to Jerusalem, not knowing what will happen to me there. I only know that in every city the Holy Spirit warns me that prison and hardships are facing me"* (Acts 20:22–23 NIV).

Paul was not worried by the Spirit's repeated warning. Even when he received confirmations and further warnings from the prophet Agabus, he continued resolutely on his way toward Jerusalem. (See Acts 21:10–15.) The word of knowledge prepared his heart and gave him courage. Sometimes a word of knowledge delivers us from a difficult situation, and sometimes it creates faith. Other times, it prepares us for the cost of what is coming; this is the mercy of God.

HOW TO RECEIVE AND RELEASE A WORD OF KNOWLEDGE

Most of the time, a word of knowledge comes to us by a quiet impression or sense. We could call this "hearing internally," or "having a gut feeling." You just "know that you know," but not how you know it. Depending on what the Holy Spirit indicates, you might share this sense with others, or you might not.

Such an internal knowing may well be confirmed by a "quickening" of a passage of Scripture, as happens with other kinds of senses from the Spirit. And sometimes, especially if the word of knowledge has to do with healing, you might receive empathetic "signals" in your own body— physical or emotional—such as a noticeable pain that you didn't have before or an oppressive feeling.

Receiving a word of knowledge is very similar to receiving a prophetic word: it can come through a vision or a dream, it can come as an audible voice, or it can come by means of an angelic visitation.

One of the most common expressions of this gift is what I would call the "spirit of counsel." A deposit of a word of knowledge is given when you are writing a letter, counseling, or praying for or about someone. The word is first received and then shared at the instigation of the Holy Spirit, and it provides godly help for the recipient. In such cases, you can see how closely it becomes allied with the gift of a word of wisdom.

Conrad of Allahabad

I was in London as part of the London Prayer Summit, and I spoke on the subject of "Gatekeepers of His Presence." As I was speaking from the podium, I glanced over to one side and felt sort of a magnetic pull toward a man with brown skin, dark hair, and dark eyes who was seated in a section some distance away, though in a seat close to the front. Weird words or syllables were floating through my mind, and I could read the syllables. It seemed like meaningless nonsense—almost like Fred Flintstone saying, "Yabba-dabba-doo"—but it persisted.

Soon, the syllables sort of gelled into "Al-la-ha-bad." Every time I looked in this man's direction, I saw those syllables in my mind. I was trying hard to deliver my message, and this was a distraction. This magnetic pull would draw my attention, and then the syllables would go through my mind. I thought it might be a message in tongues.

Eventually, I just got tired of fighting it off. I went over to that section and stood facing this fellow. I just opened my mouth and said, "Con Rod of Allahabad…. You have come from the Ganges River in India, and you have spent all the money that you had to come here to pick up the spirit of prayer because you want to take it back to a place of pilgrimage where the Hindus come and wash themselves ceremonially every year in the Ganges River." I prayed for him, and he went "out" in the Spirit.

Then I went back and completed my message. The man was still lying next to his seat when I left. It turns out that he was out for six hours straight.

The next morning, I was in the lobby of the hotel when a man came up to me and said, "How did you know my name?"

"I don't," I replied.

"Yes, you do," he countered.

"No, I don't."

We went back and forth saying yes and no. Finally he said, "Yes, you know my name, because you called it out yesterday in the meeting. It's Conrad." He pronounced his name with his proper British/Indian accent, and it sounded like "Con Rod"—not how I would normally say it with my Midwestern/Southern American accent. And he was from Allahabad, India. The rest of the information was true, too. He had miraculously received from God precisely what he had come for, through prayer based on a word of knowledge.

Daniel from Schenectady, and Twelve Elizabeths

Another time, I was ministering in Long Island, and the Holy Spirit gave me the name "Daniel" and also "Schenectady." I did not know where Schenectady, New York, was, and I wasn't even sure how to pronounce it. The Spirit told me, *Yes, there is one Daniel here tonight who is from Schenectady. And there will be twelve Elizabeths here tonight.*

Okay, I said silently, and then I spoke into the microphone, "Where is Daniel?"

Daniel, of course, is a pretty common name. There could have been ten Daniels in that big place. Only one Daniel stood up. "Sir, you are from Schenectady, New York" (and I said it correctly). The presence of God came on him, and the Spirit began to work in his body and heart.

Then I moved on to the Elizabeths. "Twelve Elizabeths are here tonight, and [the Spirit put this in my mind at that moment] God wants to heal each of you of the same ailment." Twelve women named Elizabeth came to the front, all of whom had the same need for healing—and they all received a special touch from the Lord. The simple but specific word of knowledge led straight to healing faith.

HOW TO OPERATE IN THE GIFT OF A WORD OF KNOWLEDGE

When a word of knowledge is accurate, it is a wonderful thing. But if you speak something that is not actually a word of knowledge, it can be embarrassing, at the least, if not downright damaging to people. If you feel that God wants you to use this gift, it is important to heed the following important advice.

As with the gift of prophecy, the best way to grow and develop a reliable track record is to submit your words for discernment to someone in authority over you. This person can help you to confirm, to disconfirm, or to fine-tune the words. I did this for a long time when I was a beginning prophet, and it was vital to my learning curve. Whenever I got a word, a vision, or a dream, I would write down everything about my experience before delivering it anywhere. I would highlight certain parts of my account and say, "This is simply an impression," or "This carried a very intense presence of God," and then I would submit the written account for review. Many of these words never actually got delivered to anyone, because sometimes I "missed it" and other times someone else delivered the word ahead of me. (God does that.) All of it was excellent practice in honing my ability to interpret what I received—and in giving me a feel for how and when to deliver a word. I considered it an important part of my "on-the-job" training.

Remember that a word of knowledge is not necessarily complete in itself. You will need wisdom (received directly from God or through the counsel of another) to know what to do. It is all-important to respect the other members of the body around you. We all need to walk with each other and to build a history together. No one person should be a star.

Do not talk too much. Excessive verbiage almost always stems from insecurity. Make it a priority to find your security in God's love, not in human adulation. At the same time, do not be afraid to speak out. Step out in faith, because that is the only way to learn the ropes. Be flat-out tenacious about growing in your gifts. *"Make every effort,"* as Peter said:

> *Make every effort to add to your faith goodness; and to goodness, knowledge; and to knowledge, self-control; and to self-control, perseverance; and to perseverance, godliness; and to godliness, mutual affection; and to mutual affection, love. For if you possess these qualities in increasing measure, they will keep you from being ineffective and unproductive in your knowledge of our Lord Jesus Christ.* (2 Peter 1:5–8 NIV)

Using your gifts is part of growing in holiness, and growing in holiness enhances your use of God's gifts. Learn from your mistakes and mature in all things having to do with Christ Jesus. Whatever you do, never quit! Practice *will* bring you into maturity.

Even if a word of knowledge never gets delivered, it can inform intercessory prayer. As always, humility matters. You may never have the honor of speaking out a word of knowledge or prophecy, but that is not the kind of honor you should desire, anyway. *Honor lies in God trusting you.* Believers' spheres of influence and their effectiveness will never be identical. Your special sphere might be a particular congregation, your favorite coffee shop, your workplace, or your family. Just be faithful to the Lord and to whatever words He gives you, wherever He gives them, and God will reward your faithfulness with true spiritual riches.

In the fall of 2014, the Holy Spirit gave me a dream on the Day of Atonement. In the dream, I heard, "The seeds of the seers and prophets from a generation ago have now come into fruition and maturity. Therefore, I will release once again the detailed word of knowledge, creating an atmosphere of the fear of the Lord, awe, and wonder." Along with that word from the Lord, I was given two dreams that same night concerning a "next generation" leader in California named Shawn Bolz. I knew Shawn, as he had been my student in Kansas City when he was only twenty years old. It was now twenty years later! In these two dreams, I saw the Holy Spirit's spotlight resting on him and setting him apart as a forerunner for his generation, operating in a gift of an increasingly detailed word of knowledge. In the dream, I was laying hands on him, acknowledging this; I seemed to be a part of commissioning him. Well, the dream has come true! That following January, at the annual Harvest International prophetic conference in Pasadena, California, I participated in commissioning Shawn into this sphere. Today, he is moving in a consistent manner, revealing precise details about people's lives, such as birth dates, names, street addresses, and much more, as he ministers to them.

The gift of a word of knowledge is not for only a special few. You and I can regularly expect words of knowledge to weave through our daily lives. How gracious of the Spirit to give us glimpses of His comprehensive understanding. May we learn to spot words of knowledge so that we can use them appropriately—and so we can thank the Giver of the gift. May the gift of a word of knowledge increase in our midst!

Gracious Father, we are honored to be called Your sons and daughters in these difficult times in which we live. We need Your help. So, I am asking for an increase of the gift of a word of knowledge, along with Your wisdom. You have promised that there would be an increase of the detailed gift of a word of knowledge in this day and age. I posture myself to be among those who receive and release words of knowledge for encouragement, healings, miracles, signs, and wonders. It is all for Your glory! I am expecting to receive from You right now. In Jesus' name, amen.

SECTION THREE

POWER GIFTS—THE GIFTS THAT DO

*S*ection three deals with the gifts that "do," or what we might call the supernatural power gifts. We begin in chapter 7 with the gift of faith. I emphasize that this gift is not *our* faith—it is an impartation of a portion of *God's* faith. That is why it carries with it such confidence and authority. The spiritual gift of faith is like faith with a booster rocket. It is a supernatural confidence-surge that makes it possible for a person to pray or declare God's will and thereby see it done.

The gift of faith enables a believer to speak change-producing words directly to a person, an object, or a situation—or to God on behalf of a person, an object, or a situation. The "faith surge" carries with it the method of execution that is appropriate.

In chapter 8, I unwrap the gifts of healings. There are so many needs for healing, and so many different ways to address them. Not only do people need physical healing for all kinds of ailments and disabilities, but they also need psychological healing, emotional healing, and spiritual healing.

Sometimes healings happen gradually, sometimes instantaneously. In this chapter, I seek to show you how healing works and the variety of ways healing can come to the person in need. I also emphasize that where healing is concerned, we need to be sure to align ourselves with God's timing. Finally, I encourage those who are in earnest about wanting to be able to receive and release gifts of healings to sit under the ministries of some of the modern heroes of the faith.

In chapter 9, we explore the workings of miracles. Healings can sometimes be spectacular, but miracles are even more impressive. One reason is that miracles appear to disregard the laws of nature. Healings can happen naturally in some cases, and divine healing just speeds them up. But miracles always go beyond the natural. As I continue to emphasize throughout the book, these extraordinary gifts are given by the Spirit and are never the result of our human ability. I like how Dick Iverson puts it: the gift is "the God-given ability to cooperate with God as He performs miracles."

At the end of this chapter, I emphasize that God's purpose for the workings of miracles—and all of the gifts—is to build up His kingdom. To that end, He builds up the people who populate His kingdom, and He exalts His glory through miraculous works so that more people will come to believe in Him and follow Him.

7

THE GIFT OF FAITH

"Then the disciples came to Jesus in private and asked, 'Why couldn't we drive it out?' He replied, 'Because you have so little faith. Truly I tell you, if you have faith as small as a mustard seed, you can say to this mountain, "Move from here to there," and it will move. Nothing will be impossible for you.'"
—Matthew 17:19–20 (NIV)

We need the gift of faith to be fully operational in the church and in our lives today and every day. Faith *is*. Faith is not about yesterday or even some time in the future. To receive and release this precious commodity called the gift of faith, you have to be living in the present-tense, "now" moment of time.

"Put on the full armor of God" (Ephesians 6:11), Paul wrote to the members of the church in Ephesus. His advice applies to every single member

of the body of Christ; that means each one of us must wear every piece of spiritual armor daily. (See Ephesians 6:14–18.) As an important part of that full armor, well-equipped Christians carry a *"shield of faith"* (verse 16). Without the shield of faith, we become casualties on the battlefield. With it, we can extinguish the fiery arrows of the evil one, as well as help to shield our fellow soldiers. But we must take it up and use it. We must exercise our measure of faith—*faithfully* (in both senses of the word). Again, Jude exhorted us, *"But you, beloved, build yourselves up on your most holy faith"* (Jude 1:20 NRSV).

The starting point is the basic faith that every believer must take up daily. We call it our *"measure of faith"* (Romans 12:3; see also Romans 14:1–2; Ephesians 4:12–13). When our measure of faith is exercised faithfully, it grows, and it bears abundant fruit. It may start out very small, but it can accomplish great things. Jesus said, *"Truly I tell you, if you have faith as small as a mustard seed, you can say to this mountain, 'Move from here to there,' and it will move. Nothing will be impossible for you."*

But your "faith muscles" will never get built up if you do not use your shield. If you have a spectator faith—you love to watch *others* exercise their faith—then you will become a couch-potato Christian. You have been born with the same basic set of physical muscles as everyone else, but if you do not exercise your muscles, you will become puny instead of strong. On the spiritual battlefield, how much you exercise your faith will determine how big your "guns" are.

If you are truly "faith-full," you will be filled with two kinds of faith: faith in God's ability to do amazing things, and faithfulness, as in dependability. The latter kind is a character trait, an attribute of a person of covenant loyalty, whose word is bond. *"The fruit of the Spirit is…faithfulness"* (Galatians 5:22).

Both kinds of basic faith should continue growing over time, but that can happen only with consistent use. Everyone's faith works—and grows—through love. *"For in Christ Jesus neither circumcision nor uncircumcision means anything, but faith working through love"* (Galatians 5:6). Isn't wonderful how all of the fruit and attributes of God and His gifts work together? I just love Him and His ways!

DEFINING THE GIFT OF FAITH

It can sometimes be difficult to differentiate the spiritual gift of faith from the measure of faith that is common to every believer (without which we could not even come to a saving faith). The late Kenneth Hagin, the father of the Word of Faith movement, said that the gift of faith is "special faith." It is different from saving faith; additionally, it is separate from faithfulness as a fruit of the Spirit. He wrote, "The gift of faith is a gift of the Spirit to the believer in order that he might *receive* miracles.... Those who operate in special faith, the gift of the Spirit, can believe God in such a way that *God* honors their word as His own, and miraculously brings to pass the desired result."[1]

Additionally, Dick Iverson explains the gift in this way:

The gift of faith is the God-given ability to believe Him for the impossible in a particular situation. It is not so much the general faith which believes God for provision, but goes a step beyond, where one *just knows* that a particular thing is the will of God and is going to happen.[2]

The spiritual gift of faith is like faith with a booster rocket. It is a supernatural confidence-surge that makes it possible for a person to pray or declare God's will and to thereby effect either miraculous blessings or cursing and destruction.[3] (We would prefer to think only of the blessings and creative miracles, but remember that faith power can also toss mountains into the sea or wither fig trees within hours; see Mark 11:12–14, 20–24.)

The spiritual gift of faith is not *your* faith—it is an impartation of a portion of *God's* faith. That is why it carries with it such confidence and authority, as we see in this passage:

And Jesus answered saying to them, "Have faith in God. Truly I say to you, whoever says to this mountain, 'Be taken up and cast into the sea,' and does not doubt in his heart, but believes that what he says is going to happen, it will be granted him." (Mark 11:22–23)

Let me add one more point: We have been given a huge key to moving in this amazing dimension of the gift of faith—forgiveness. Forgiveness is essential for any kind of faith to flourish, including faith that is imparted as a gift. We know this because almost immediately after Jesus taught about having faith enough to make a mountain throw itself into the ocean, He said, *"Whenever you stand praying, forgive, if you have anything against anyone, so that your Father who is in heaven will also forgive you your transgressions"* (Mark 11:25). The flow of faith will be interrupted by hardheartedness, but forgiveness can remove blockages to faith. Forgiveness from the heart opens the door both ways—to receive and to release the gifts of the Holy Spirit. So you see that the importance of forgiveness cannot be overstated!

THE GIFT OF FAITH IN ACTION

Peter exercised a gift of faith when he and John encountered the lame beggar at the temple gate called Beautiful:

> *Now Peter and John were going up to the temple at the ninth hour, the hour of prayer. And a man who had been lame from his mother's womb was being carried along, whom they used to set down every day at the gate of the temple which is called Beautiful, in order to beg alms of those who were entering the temple. When he saw Peter and John about to go into the temple, he began asking to receive alms. But Peter, along with John, fixed his gaze on him and said, "Look at us!" And he began to give them his attention, expecting to receive something from them. But Peter said, "I do not possess silver and gold, but what I do have I give to you: In the name of Jesus Christ the Nazarene—walk!" And seizing him by the right hand, he raised him up; and immediately his feet and his ankles were strengthened. With a leap he stood upright and began to walk; and he entered the temple with them, walking and leaping and praising God. And all the people saw him walking and praising God; and they were taking note of him as being the one who used to sit at the Beautiful Gate of the temple to beg alms, and they were filled with wonder and amazement at what had happened to him.* (Acts 3:1–10)

As soon as Peter saw the lame beggar, he knew that the man would be healed. He proclaimed his healing with unflinching and unwavering faith, and then took him by the hand to lift him to his feet. First he had to get the man's attention away from begging and money. *"Look at us!"* he instructed him. Peter locked eyes with the man, and there was a heart-to-heart exchange through their eyes. The man's expectation rose, probably only for a generous handout, but Peter's faith brought him a miracle instead. This man, who had never before stood up on his own feet, found himself not only standing but also walking and leaping with joy. Of course, he would now have to find a new way to earn a living instead of begging, but he didn't worry about that. Peter's gift of faith had opened the way to a whole new life.

Jesus—who possesses all of the spiritual gifts because they emanate from Him—continually exercised the gift of faith while He lived on earth. Before He raised Lazarus from the dead (see John 11), He delayed going to visit Martha and Mary at their brother's tomb, but this actually demonstrated His faith. Jesus had rock-solid faith; He knew that this seeming defeat would be turned into unqualified victory. He was moved to tears by the grief that surrounded the family, because Lazarus was one of His best friends, and it seems to me that He could have slipped into further grieving, but He rose above it and didn't waste any time. Similarly, the atmosphere of unbelief that surrounded the tomb could have drawn off His faith like a ground wire, which taps off the flow of current from a lightning strike, but He didn't let that happen. Instead, He exhorted Martha to have faith, saying, *"Did I not say to you that if you believe, you will see the glory of God?"* (John 11:40), and then boldly called Lazarus out of the tomb, alive.

PRACTICAL APPLICATIONS OF THE GIFT OF FAITH

This dimension of faith leaves no room for doubt. It lays hold of the will of God for a situation despite any opposition. When the gift of faith is surging, nothing can stand in its way. It moves mountains!

Today, many of us have learned to walk in the amazing realm of faith. Only God could display His power through such a diversity of gifts and operations of those gifts through the many members of the body of Christ. My own faith tends to come most fully alive in times of crisis intervention through intercession; and as a result of prayers coupled with welling faith, I have seen history changed before my very eyes. My friend James Maloney moves in the gift of faith unto miracles in possibly one of the most highly consistent ways of anyone today. When he prays for people who have had metal pins surgically implanted into their bodies, the people are healed—and the metal pins, no longer needed to support a shattered bone, just disappear, time after time!

This is not to say that a person with the gift of faith possesses the same level of faith for every circumstance. As with the other spiritual gifts, the gift of faith seems to "specialize." One person's faith emphasis, like mine, could be faith for crisis intervention through intercession. Another person's sphere of influence might be faith for finances or for miracles. I have seen people with gifts of faith that are specific to severe weather patterns, healing, evangelism, and deliverance from evil spirits, and none of those people would find their gift operational outside of their sphere of influence. At times, the operation of the gift appears to be determined according to the presenting need or to a person's function within the body of Christ. When this happens, the gift of faith operates independent of someone's identity as a gifted person; it is faith for special miracles or for acts that God wants to perform in given circumstances.

For some people, the influence of the gift of faith is funneled into individual ministries that might be better known by the names of other spiritual gifts; in this case, the gift of faith performs a very specific support role. We can glimpse this interconnectedness of gifts in the following passage of Scripture:

> *Since we have gifts that differ according to the grace given to us, each of us is to exercise them accordingly: if prophecy, according to the proportion of his faith; if service, in his serving; or he who teaches, in his teaching; or he who exhorts, in his exhortation; he who gives, with liberality; he who leads, with diligence; he who shows mercy, with cheerfulness.*
> (Romans 12:6–8)

"*According to the proportion of his faith.*" These gifts complement one another; they never compete with each other. In fact, one gift leads to another gift being activated and released. There is a divine cooperation within the

Godhead that creates a "no-competition zone," and we need to learn to model this cooperation in the body of Christ!

Whatever the focus, the gift of faith enables a person to speak change-producing words directly to a person, an object, or a situation—or to God on behalf of a person, an object, or a situation. The "faith surge" carries with it the method of execution that is appropriate. Out of a gift of faith, Elijah declared, in God's name, that no rain would fall in Israel, and then, after a long time of severe drought, he announced the return of the rain. (See 1 Kings 17:1; 18:1, 41–45; see also James 5:17–18.) On behalf of God, Joshua spoke to the sun and the moon, telling them to stand still to enable the Israelites to win a decisive battle against their enemies. (See Joshua 10:12–14.) Jesus spoke to the wind and the waves to calm a fierce storm. (See, for example, Luke 8:23–25.)

It might seem to be arrogant on the part of the speaker to utter such commands, but if God is behind the words through the gift of faith, the speaker is humbled by them. The speaker knows full well that his or her words alone have no power at all and in fact may sound rather foolish if God doesn't back them up with results. Thus, the empowerment of the Holy Spirit must be the motivating force behind the words that we speak.

WHAT I RECEIVED THROUGH A MAN WITH THE GIFT OF FAITH

You may know my life story, how I went through eight or nine years (three recurrences) of non-Hodgkin's lymphoma, a kind of cancer. It seemed to hide and then creep back, but I beat it twice. Then it came back a third time. I did everything I could, using every method and integrating every healing approach that I knew. I wanted to live and not die!

I had just undergone an intense treatment at the top integrated-cancer-treatment center in the United States, and as a result, my immune system was significantly weakened and my white blood count was extremely low. I had to wear a white mask, and I was semi-quarantined. Then I heard that ninety-year-old Oral Roberts, the fabled faith-healing evangelist, was hosting small groups of leaders once a month, by invitation only, at his home in

Orange County, California. I received one of those precious invitations in September 2009, just when I needed it. I thought, *If I can just get on a plane and get there, I might just be the last person in Oral Roberts' life that he lays hands on and who gets to receive the assurance that they have been healed of cancer.*

So I got my airline ticket. The next thing I knew, I was in the living room of this patriarch of the faith who had seen the healing revival movement of the twentieth century. There with me were Bill Johnson and other leaders from across the nation. At the close of the gathering, my turn for prayer came. I sat on a stool in front of Oral's chair, and he laid his experienced hands upon me for about fifteen seconds and declared, "I command every cancer cell in this man's body to dry up and never come back again!" It felt as if a lightning bolt had struck me, and a surge of faith was deposited within me.

Now I can announce that the cancer has never come back since, and I believe that it never will. And I can attest to the fact that the gift of faith works! Oral Roberts graduated to his heavenly award that following December. I am forever grateful for that opportunity to be ministered to by him!

A "GENERAL" OF FAITH

We can be encouraged to exercise our faith by hearing stories about the great "generals" of faith who have gone before us. One of those generals is Smith Wigglesworth. He was born in Yorkshire, England, in 1859, and he graduated to glory in 1947. Wigglesworth became known as the "apostle of faith," but he started out as an unschooled plumber. He did not even learn to read until after he married his wife, Polly, a preacher in the Salvation Army, in 1882, and he learned by reading the Bible.

Faith was the primary gifting in his life and ministry. One day, he came home from work and found that his dear wife had died a couple of hours earlier. What did he do? He responded out of pure faith, standing her dead body up against a wall and declaring a word of faith to her dead corpse. He commanded Polly to come back to life, and she did! She lived for some years after that.[4]

Many people claimed that they were healed of cancer through his ministry, and testimonies appeared in Pentecostal magazines of miraculous results that came from Wigglesworth's unusually strong faith. Admittedly, he sometimes operated in an unorthodox manner that created some controversy—such as punching the diseased part of a person's body as he prayed. But no one could argue with his results. Miracles happened year after year. His ministry took him across Europe and into Southeast Asia, the United States, and Africa. Some of his inspiring sermons and stories are preserved for us in the books *Ever Increasing Faith* and *Faith That Prevails*. God did it before, and He is more than ready and able to do that in our day!

MORE DESIRABLE THAN GOLD

When God reveals certain facts concerning His will in a circumstance, and you "just know" it will happen, that is the gift of faith. It is to be much sought after. Such faith is irresistible. When such knowledge is declared orally, the words do not return void. (See Isaiah 55:11.) *"They are more desirable than gold"*:

> *The commandment of the LORD is pure, enlightening the eyes. The fear of the LORD is clean, enduring forever; the judgments of the LORD are true; they are righteous altogether. They are more desirable than gold, yes, than much fine gold; sweeter also than honey and the drippings of the honeycomb.* (Psalm 19:8–10)

God gives the gift of faith generously, and He wants us to recognize when we experience it, so that we will appreciate it and use it well and wisely. Let's all make a point to use the measure of faith with which we have been supplied, rejoicing greatly should our circumstances or our sphere of influence require more. Let's lay hold of God and let His faith be deposited within each of us in ever-increasing measure!

Dear Lord, I thank You for the measure of faith we each receive, and I am grateful for the opportunity to grow in the fruit of the

Spirit called *faithfulness*. But I want more, Lord! Release the gift of faith into my life to bring forth miracles for the glory of Christ Jesus' holy name in the earth. Romans 10:17 says that "*faith comes from hearing, and hearing by the word of Christ.*" So, I vow to store up the words of God in my heart as a way of positioning myself to grow in faith. I want to speak to mountains in Jesus' great name and see them move! "More love, more power, more of You in my life."[5] Amen!

8

THE GIFTS OF HEALINGS

"As Peter traveled about the country, he went to visit the Lord's people who lived in Lydda. There he found a man named Aeneas, who was paralyzed and had been bedridden for eight years. 'Aeneas,' Peter said to him, 'Jesus Christ heals you. Get up and roll up your mat.' Immediately Aeneas got up. All those who lived in Lydda and Sharon saw him and turned to the Lord."
—Acts 9:32–35 (NIV)

efore I get this chapter underway, I want to point out that we're not going to be looking at the "gift of healing." Instead, we'll be surveying more than one gift. Interestingly, in his list of spiritual gifts in 1 Corinthians 12, Paul wrote it as "gifts" of "healings." If you look at the original Greek wording, both words, "gift" and "healing," are plural, and they lack the definite article, as indicated in the *New King James* translation:

> *There are diversities of gifts, but the same Spirit.... For to one is given...**gifts of healings** by the same Spirit.... God has appointed these in the church: first apostles, second prophets, third teachers, after that miracles, then **gifts of healings**, helps, administrations, varieties of tongues.... Do all have **gifts of healings**?*
>
> (1 Corinthians 12:4, 8–9, 28, 30 NKJV)

"Gifts of healings" is a perfect way to describe spiritual healing, which encompasses a multiplicity of applications. There are so many needs for healing, and so many different ways to address them. Not only do people need physical healing for all kinds of ailments and disabilities, but they also need psychological healing, emotional healing, and spiritual healing. Healings sometimes happen gradually, sometimes instantaneously. Healings can happen after a word of personal prayer or a faith-filled declaration, but sometimes they occur because of the spiritual atmosphere of a group setting.

Once again, I turn to my friend Sam Storms, as he sees a strong correlation between the gifts of healings and the gift of faith, which is listed immediately before the gifts of healings in Paul's list from 1 Corinthians 12. In his book *The Beginner's Guide to Spiritual Gifts*, he wrote,

> Evidently Paul did not envision that a person would be endowed with one healing gift operative at all times for all diseases. His language suggests either many different gifts or powers of healing, each appropriate to and effective for its related illness, or each occurrence of healing constituting a distinct gift in its own right.[1]

People whose gifts include healing vary in personality, position, and circumstances and thus minister divine healing in many different ways, developing many viable models for using gifts of healing. Healing is never a one-size-fits-all gift. Here's a quick snapshot of healing models drawn from my own ministry experience. Influenced by Kenneth Hagin and Benny Hinn (who prayed for me more than once for impartations of God's power), I first learned to declare healing straightforwardly, essentially using the Word of Faith method. Then I was exposed to the third-wave healing model developed by John Wimber, his widely used, five-stage (interview/

interactive) approach. On the heels of that came the "Toronto Blessing" outpouring of the Holy Spirit, emphasizing "soaking"—waiting, worshipping, and resting in the Spirit as an avenue for healing. This was followed by the Sozo healing model (*sozo* is the Greek word for "salvation"), which in some circles overlaps with what is called Freedom Prayer.

Along the way, I also came to appreciate the Elijah House method, developed by John and Paula Sanford to address the psychological and emotional components of physical healing. I became dear friends with Cal Pierce, who heads up the modern-day Healing Rooms (originated by John G. Lake). But possibly the most comprehensive approach that I am aware of has been developed by Chester and Betsy Kylstra of Restoring The Foundations.

As you can see, there have been many advancements in the body of Christ concerning gifts of healings, and I have had a big learning curve in my own personal life in regard to them, as well. I have attended countless healing conferences and ministered alongside gifted leaders over the years and have seen the founding of a number of schools of healing and the supernatural in conjunction with vibrant churches and ministry centers, along with houses of healing, healing rooms, and more. With health challenges of my own, I have learned to maximize health and healing through certain liturgical practices, such as taking Communion regularly, and I continue to benefit from the combined wisdom of nutritional and lifestyle advice and keeping the Sabbath rest.

It is not hard to see that God's people need healing from all kinds of disorders and infirmities that require being approached in all kinds of ways. This is why Paul's plural terminology "gifts of healings" is spot-on. It is always the same Spirit of Jesus who performs the healing. But through human intermediaries, He presents Himself in different "packages" for different people at different times in different situations.

GIFTS OF HEALINGS DEFINED

As I said earlier, healing—even supernatural healing—is not always instantaneous. At times, it may seem more natural than miraculous. Its many expressions of operation can involve more than one working of God's grace. But in every instance, gifts of healings relieve human bodies of disease, disability, or sickness[2]; and the gifts operate under God's control.[3]

People who use their gifts of healings for the benefit of others are rarely trained as medical professionals (although they may be). As Kenneth Hagin pointed out, "The healing that is supernatural doesn't come by diagnosis or by prescribing treatment. Divine healing comes by laying on of hands, anointing with oil, or sometimes just by speaking the Word, just to name a few examples from the Word of how healing is ministered."[4] People with gifts of healings may see obvious results instantly, or they may find it difficult to pinpoint people's improvement. Gifts of healings may be said to speed up the process of healing in a sick person (which may or may not be feasible without the supernatural boost). If for no other reason, the wide variety of healing gifts is needed to address the many kinds of illnesses that people suffer from.[5]

As far as spiritual gifts are concerned, this particular one reaches out to grab your attention. Everyone needs divine healing at some point in their lives, and it is good to know that you do not have to follow a strict formula in order to be healed. Divine healing is a very real prospect, not just some kind of quackery offered by charlatans.

HOW GIFTS OF HEALINGS WORK

The members of the body of Christ have learned to use their gifts of healings first from the teaching and example of the New Testament, and second, predictably, from accumulated experience.

Scriptural accounts show us that there is just as much precedent for a healing that unfolds in stages or over time as for an instantaneous miracle. For example, when Jesus prayed for a blind man (after spitting on his eyes!—an example no one should follow without specific divine guidance) his sight returned only after a second effort. (See Mark 8:22–25.) Jesus spat and prayed the first time, and queried him, *"Do you see anything?"* (Mark 8:23). The man could see, but only vaguely. So Jesus prayed and spat on his eyes again, after which his vision was perfect.

"Slow" healings are no less real than instant ones, of course, but we find the immediate ones to be more exciting, such as the following examples. Jesus said to a leper, *"'Be cleansed.' **Immediately** his leprosy was cleansed"* (Matthew 8:3 NKJV). One moment, Simon's mother-in-law was in bed with a fever, but the next moment, she had been healed by Jesus, and she was waiting on Jesus, her son-in-law, and the others who had come with them to her house. (See Mark 1:30–31.)

Instant healings can occur even when the person who prays or declares a healing is not physically with the person who is ill. In one notable incident, a royal official had a son who was near death, and he begged Jesus to come and heal the boy. Jesus was able to speak a word of healing at a distance that was just as effective as if He had touched the sick person.

> *The royal official said, "Sir, come down before my child dies." "Go,"*
> *Jesus replied, "your son will live." The man took Jesus at his word and*
> *departed. While he was still on the way, his servants met him with the*
> *news that his boy was living. When he inquired as to the time when his*
> *son got better, they said to him, "Yesterday, at one in the afternoon, the*
> *fever left him."* (John 4:49–52 NIV)

This account shows us the raw power of a word of healing when Jesus initiates it. Remember also the story of the centurion's slave, told in Luke 7:2–10. It doesn't matter whether people request healing on their own behalf; whether someone brings them for healing (as happens often in the case of children or severely disabled ones); or if someone comes as an intermediary, seeking only a word of healing for another, as the centurion did. Often enough, the person who needs healing does not even seek it out at all, or requires some gentle persuasion to accept the idea. Recall the lame man at the pool of Bethesda:

> *After these things there was a feast of the Jews, and Jesus went up to*
> *Jerusalem. Now there is in Jerusalem by the sheep gate a pool, which is*
> *called in Hebrew Bethesda, having five porticoes. In these lay a multi-*
> *tude of those who were sick, blind, lame, and withered, [waiting for the*
> *moving of the waters; for an angel of the Lord went down at certain*
> *seasons into the pool and stirred up the water; whoever then first, after*

the stirring up of the water, stepped in was made well from whatever disease with which he was afflicted.] A man was there who had been ill for thirty-eight years. When Jesus saw him lying there, and knew that he had already been a long time in that condition, He said to him, "Do you wish to get well?" The sick man answered Him, "Sir, I have no man to put me into the pool when the water is stirred up, but while I am coming, another steps down before me." Jesus said to him, "Get up, pick up your pallet and walk." Immediately the man became well, and picked up his pallet and began to walk. (John 5:1–9)

Where healing is concerned, we need to be sure to align ourselves with God's timing. Remember how Jesus delayed before He went to raise Lazarus from the dead. Evidently, it would not have been good enough to heal Lazarus' life-threatening sickness. Instead, He waited until it was "too late" so that He could perform a much more spectacular kind of healing— a resurrection.

I remember one time when I had a strong sense of timing for healing prayer. A friend of mine was hospitalized, and I was called to come because he was so sick. However, rather than jumping into the car to hurry to the hospital, I felt restrained by the Holy Spirit. The fact that the sick one was my dear friend made the waiting even harder. All I felt free to do was to minister to the Lord (pray and worship and wait for His timing) at home. After about a day and a half, it seemed okay to go to the hospital. All I knew was that my friend was now in worse shape than ever, but I was undeterred by that because now I had faith exploding in my heart. When I went into my friend's hospital room, he was in a coma and tubes were everywhere. I started thumping on his chest, and suddenly the gauges started showing activity, and he began to revive. Before long, he was released from the hospital, totally healed. His dear wife declared it a miracle; all I know is that I listened and obeyed, and God showed up!

Laying on of Hands

Many, many times, healing occurs when someone lays his or her hands on the one who needs healing. Jesus and the members of the early church used this practice all the time. The following is a sampling of Scriptures regarding the laying on of hands for healing:

At sunset, the people brought to Jesus all who had various kinds of sickness, and laying his hands on each one, he healed them.

(Luke 4:40 NIV)

And it happened that the father of Publius was lying in bed afflicted with recurrent fever and dysentery; and Paul went in to see him and after he had prayed, he laid his hands on him and healed him. After this had happened, the rest of the people on the island who had diseases were coming to him and getting cured.　　　　(Acts 28:8–9)

These signs will accompany those who have believed:…they will lay hands on the sick, and they will recover.　　　　(Mark 16:17–18)

Praying for the sick with the laying on of hands is not meant only for individuals who have been given gifts of healings. It's the prerogative of all "believing believers" to have faith in God's Word and pray for the sick. Sometimes, the laying on of hands includes anointing with oil, and often the anointing is done by a church leader. Here is the scriptural precedent for that:

Is anyone among you sick? Then he must call for the elders of the church and they are to pray over him, anointing him with oil in the name of the Lord; and the prayer offered in faith will restore the one who is sick, and the Lord will raise him up, and if he has committed sins, they will be forgiven him.　　　　(James 5:14–15)

And they [the twelve disciples] were casting out many demons and were anointing with oil many sick people and healing them.　　　　(Mark 6:13)

Occasionally (although this delivery method of healing has been abused), something other than hands can be laid on the sick, such as an item of clothing from an anointed person or even the shadow of someone who has a healing gift. These form a point of contact for the one in need. The following account took place after Jesus had been teaching publicly and performing miracles for a while, and His reputation had begun to precede Him.

When they got out of the boat, immediately the people recognized Him, and ran about that whole country and began to carry here and there on their pallets those who were sick, to the place they heard He was. Wherever He entered villages, or cities, or countryside, they were laying the sick in the market places, and imploring Him that they might just touch the fringe of His cloak; and as many as touched it were being cured. (Mark 6:54–56)

Later, a similar thing happened with Peter and the other apostles:

At the hands of the apostles many signs and wonders were taking place among the people; and they were all with one accord in Solomon's portico.… [People] even carried the sick out into the streets and laid them on cots and pallets, so that when Peter came by at least his shadow might fall on any one of them. Also the people from the cities in the vicinity of Jerusalem were coming together, bringing people who were sick or afflicted with unclean spirits, and they were all being healed. (Acts 5:12, 15–16)

In Ephesus, Paul performed *"extraordinary miracles,"* some of which were *extra*-extraordinary because they occurred by means of items of his clothing, without Paul being present. (These miracles must have happened in this way either due to direct revelation about them or because there was no other way for Paul to lay his hands on all of the sick people in the region.)

God was performing extraordinary miracles by the hands of Paul, so that handkerchiefs or aprons were even carried from his body to the sick, and the diseases left them and the evil spirits went out. (Acts 19:11–12)

(Lest you picture Paul wearing a cravat or a bandanna-type handkerchief along with a contemporary ladies' kitchen apron, just remember that this probably meant his tentmaker's sweat rags and his protective craftsman's apron.) I wish I could watch a video of those diseases being healed and demons being vanquished by a little square of old cloth! In actuality, I have been in many gatherings where faith abounds and people bring handkerchiefs or items of clothing to be prayed over and then taken back to their sick loved ones. Notably, this releases an atmosphere of faith, hope, and love in which authentic healing can occur. Even when people are not healed, they often experience the special comfort of the love of God.

Recently, I observed the combined anointing of a father in the faith and his spiritual son as they ministered healing together—a generational duo. Bobby Connor, a former Baptist pastor from Texas, was joined by his spiritual son, Jerame Nelson, and they moved together in words of knowledge and gifts of healings. Two can be so much better than one. The diversity of God's ways of releasing His gifts never ceases to amaze me!

Communion—the Lord's Supper

Personally, besides direct prayer and the laying on of hands, I lean heavily on the basic healing power of the Lord's Supper (also called Communion or the Eucharist). In fact, I travel with a portable Communion kit so that I can obey the words of Jesus: *"Do this, as often as you drink it, in remembrance of Me"* (1 Corinthians 11:25). That verse doesn't say, "As seldom as you drink it," or "Once in a while." Paul wrote *"as often as you drink it"* in the context of the following familiar words:

> *For I received from the Lord that which I also delivered to you, that the Lord Jesus in the night in which He was betrayed took bread; and when He had given thanks, He broke it and said, "This is My body, which is for you; do this in remembrance of Me." In the same way He took the cup also after supper, saying, "This cup is the new covenant in My blood; do this, as often as you drink it, in remembrance of Me."*
> (1 Corinthians 11:23–25)

God has bound our physical well-being to our spiritual relationship with this "flesh and blood" aspect of His Son. We need to seek Him out, to desire His presence, to obey Him. The health of our relationship with Him and others helps to determine the health of our physical bodies:

> *Examine yourselves, and only then eat of the bread and drink of the cup. For all who eat and drink without discerning the body, eat and drink judgment against themselves. For this reason many of you are weak and ill, and some have died.* (1 Corinthians 11:28–30 NRSV)

When you partake of the Lord's Supper, you are proclaiming what the Lord has done through His death and resurrection. You receive the cleansing of forgiveness, and you forgive others. You rejoice in the fact that Jesus' blood has triumphed over the power of the Evil One. You receive and give mercy, proclaim life over yourself, and resubmit yourself to the lordship of Jesus. What could be more health-promoting than that? The Lord's Supper is the meal that heals.

Persistence Pays Off

Some healings require a lot of preliminary prayer to clear up things that impede healing. An example of this occurred one time when I was ministering with Mahesh Chavda in Haiti. Throngs of people were coming night after night, and after each meeting, we had them line up for prayer. Though the night was pitch-dark, the light of the Lord was shining brightly.

On the first night, a young girl brought to the meeting her elderly grandmother, who had been blind from birth, so that we could pray for her healing. That night, Mahesh wisely gave an invitation for salvation. The grandmother gave her life to the Lord, but she was still blind when she went home. The next night, the pair came back, and again the granddaughter brought her grandmother to stand in the line. The grandmother asked to be filled with the Holy Spirit, and she was. She was still blind, though. The third evening, we emphasized deliverance, and the two of them came forward together once again. The grandmother fell to the ground under God's power and was gloriously delivered. But when she got up, she still could not see, and her granddaughter had to lead her home by the hand in the dark of night once again.

I was amazed at the persistence and love of the little girl. The fourth night, we preached about breaking curses, and the grandmother came forward for prayer for that, also. Curses were broken, but her blindness persisted. Finally, on the fifth night, Mahesh preached about healing, and there they were again; the girl had brought her grandmother forward every night for five straight nights, regardless of the nature of the invitation, and she was not going to give up yet. That night, the old woman got healed, but we were unaware of it at first. The next thing we knew, she was up on the platform (which was the back of a flatbed truck) with the microphone, saying, "Praise the Lord" in Haitian Creole, because she was no longer blind; she could see!

Weeks later, back in the States, Mahesh was driving along the highway and thinking about the grandmother's healing. "Lord," he asked, "why didn't she get healed until the fifth time?" Immediately, he had a vision of an octopus sitting on the woman's head with its tentacle-like arms wrapped around her; every time he prayed for her, one of its arms was stripped off. The fifth time, the remaining arms were stripped off, and she received her sight. Interesting, right? It was as if layers of impediments had to be removed to get to the root of the problem so she could be healed.

The lesson? Sometimes, blind eyes can be healed in an instant, the moment they are prayed for. Other times, it takes a while—as when Jesus ministered to the blind man who saw *"men like trees, walking"* (Mark 8:24 NKJV) before he was fully restored. In any case, persistence pays off. It is so worth it to learn how to use gifts of healings.

If you are in earnest about wanting to be able to receive and release healing gifts, go sit under the ministries of some of the modern heroes of the faith, such as Randy Clark, Bill Johnson, Joan Hunter, Mahesh Chavda, James Maloney, and others. Drink in. Then do something with what you have received. Take your hands out of your pockets and put them on someone who needs healing, for Jesus' sake! Become part of the healing army for the times we live in. Turn your face from the needs for healings that clamor for your attention toward our Healer and Great Physician. Let's call forth gifts of healings for every form of sickness we know of and also for conditions we have not heard of, all for the glory of God!

⌒

Jesus, I exalt You. I know that You are the same yesterday, today, and forever, and I declare that healing is *"the children's bread,"* as You said in Matthew 15:26. Therefore, I welcome the gifts of healings into my life, into the lives of people around me, and into the ministries in my area. Come, Holy Spirit; I want more! To God be the glory, amen!

9

THE WORKINGS OF MIRACLES

*"For I will not presume to speak of anything except
what Christ has accomplished through me, resulting in
the obedience of the Gentiles by word and deed, in the power of
signs and wonders, in the power of the Spirit."*
—Romans 15:18–19

At one point during His ministry, Jesus returned to His hometown of Nazareth, but the Son of God had trouble performing miracles in its faith-deadening atmosphere: *"He could do no miracle there except that He laid His hands on a few sick people and healed them"* (Mark 6:5). His former neighbors didn't expect the bachelor Son of the local carpenter to be a miracle worker, and many of them thought He was a little bit crazy. So Jesus could not do any miracles in Nazareth, although He did heal a few sick people. Apparently, healings were easier to achieve in the face of resistance than were miracles.

Miracles go beyond healings to encompass other supernatural phenomena, including unusual meteorological happenings. Healings can sometimes be spectacular, but miracles are even more impressive. One reason is that miracles appear to disregard the laws of nature. Healings can happen naturally in some cases, and divine healing just speeds them up. But miracles? They always go beyond the natural. For example, no matter what kind of water or jars you might use, you could never change plain water into fine wine by any natural process. It would take a miracle such as Jesus performed.

> *Nearby stood six stone water jars, the kind used by the Jews for ceremonial washing, each holding from twenty to thirty gallons. Jesus said to the servants, "Fill the jars with water"; so they filled them to the brim. Then he told them, "Now draw some out and take it to the master of the banquet." They did so, and the master of the banquet tasted the water that had been turned into wine. He did not realize where it had come from, though the servants who had drawn the water knew. Then he called the bridegroom aside and said, "Everyone brings out the choice wine first and then the cheaper wine after the guests have had too much to drink; but you have saved the best till now." What Jesus did here in Cana of Galilee was the first of the signs through which he revealed his glory; and his disciples believed in him.*
>
> (John 2:6–11 NIV)

In Cana, a village a few miles from Nazareth, Jesus performed His first public miracle; and of course He went on to perform many more miracles, as did His disciples. I think it is a bit artificial to say that miracles "override" the laws of nature, as if the God who performs miracles did not set up the laws of nature in the first place. He can do whatever He wants, whenever He wants, regardless of what we consider normal and natural.

When people see a miracle, they know that something uncommon has just occurred. Their first response, like the banquet master's, is often, "I can't believe it!" But many times, the extraordinary nature of what they have just seen with their own eyes or heard with their own ears is proof positive to them that God is truly good and benevolent.

THE GIFT OF WORKINGS OF MIRACLES DEFINED

"For to one is given...the working[s] of miracles" (1 Corinthians 12:8, 10 NKJV). Similar to "gifts of healings," the original Greek would render the term plural in both parts, as "workings of miracles." The plurals indicate a range of outworkings. To be even truer to the original Greek, we could call the gift "workings of powers," because the word we translate "miracles" is *dunamis* ("powers") in Greek. The workings of miracles, then, could be understood as the "effectings" or achievements of the powers of the Holy Spirit. (See 1 Corinthians 12:10 NASB.) "The God who is always and everywhere present, upholding and sustaining and directing all things to their appointed consummation, is now [when effecting a miracle] working in a surprising and unfamiliar way," writes Sam Storms.[1]

Dick Iverson clarifies that God is the actual Miracle Worker, and that believers participate with Him in His work. The gift is "the God-given ability to cooperate with God as He performs miracles. It is actually a co-action, or joint operation; man participating with God in the performing of the impossible. It is not man performing miracles, but God performing miracles through a cooperative act with men."[2]

Is one gift of the Spirit better than another? Is one grace to be esteemed over all the rest? For sure, the "workings of powers" is one of the grace packages of the Holy Spirit that is desperately needed, and it is often the one that is the most sought after. But the best gift is always going to be the one that is needed at the moment.

Theologian and teacher Wayne Grudem defines a miracle as "a less common kind of God's activity in which he arouses people's awe and wonder and bears witness to himself."[3] This is a key feature of a real miracle. Do you think God would perform a miracle randomly and away from human notice? I don't think so. Miracles are meant to seize people's attention, to show that He is real and relevant. There is no guarantee that the people will turn wholeheartedly to God as a result, but they will be forced to think about Him. That is the effect miracles had on the Samaritan magician named Simon who followed Philip around: *"As he observed signs and great miracles taking place, he was constantly amazed"* (Acts 8:13).

THE WILL OF GOD PLUS HUMAN OBEDIENCE

If you examine a miracle, you will almost always find that it was sparked by someone's simple act of obedience. The miraculous results are all the more outstanding in comparison to the initial act of faith. When God parted the Red Sea for the Israelites, Moses' job was not strenuous. God told him to lift up his staff and stretch out his hand over the sea. (See Exodus 14:16.) Later, when Moses and the people arrived at Marah where the waters were too bitter to drink, the Lord told Moses to throw a particular tree into the pool of water, and by a miracle the water became sweet. (See Exodus 15:23–25.) In both cases, Moses had to follow through. Neither the staff nor the tree caused the miracle; the miracle was effected by the power of God. But Moses had to obey explicitly. If he had shouted at the sea instead of raising his hand and his staff over it, it is quite possible that the Egyptians would have caught up with them. If he had slipped the tree into the water quietly (or if he had tossed in his staff as a substitute) instead of throwing the designated tree in with a big splash, the Israelites' drinking water would most likely have remained bitter.

In other words, Moses committed himself to act according to what the Lord told him. Faith is not tentative. Obedience is not an experiment. It is a real commitment, and it may involve performing a seemingly ridiculous act in front of multitudes of people.

Obedience is preceded by a communication from God. Obedient faith comes from hearing: *"So faith comes from hearing, and hearing by the word of Christ"* (Romans 10:17). In the above instances, God told Moses what to do. Likewise, the Spirit directed the prophet Ezekiel to the valley of the dry bones, and then He instructed the prophet what to say and do. (See Ezekiel 37:1–10.) The Lord told the prophet Elijah to give a destitute widow an unlikely-sounding word of direction, and her small supply of oil multiplied to fill every last jar she had collected. (See 2 Kings 4:1–7.) Miracles occur by believing and acting on the word of the Lord.

God is the only uncreated Being in the universe, having created everything else that has ever existed. *"By the word of the LORD the heavens were made, and by the breath of His mouth all their host"* (Psalm 33:6). God the Son—the Word made flesh—*"upholds all things by the word [rhema, Greek] of His power"* (Hebrews 1:3). He upholds all things by the *rhema*, or spoken word, that He utters. We see that through Jesus' spoken words, and those of His followers in His name, miracles were effected. (See, for example, John 5:8–9; John 11:43–44; Acts 3:6–8.)

Still, you can have all the divine words that you want, but unless obedient acts of faith accompany the spoken word of the Lord, nothing can happen. *"So faith by itself, if it has no works, is dead"* (James 2:17 NRSV). The only way the mountain can be cast into the sea is by faith—faith that stands firm, without a flicker of doubt: *"Truly I say to you, whoever says to this mountain, 'Be taken up and cast into the sea,' and does not doubt in his heart, but believes that what he says is going to happen, it will be granted him"* (Mark 11:23).

MIRACLES FREELY GIVEN

Always remember, miracles are gifts. You do not earn them. You cannot perform well enough to deserve them. They are given freely by the Holy Spirit, and like all of His gifts, they are demonstrations of the depths of God's immense love. The spiritual gifts are given to flow through us as acts of mercy, kindness, and love toward others. In other words, we cannot hoard them and keep them to ourselves. These grace packages are meant to pass through our hands; we are to distribute them as God shows us. Freely we have received, now freely we give! (See Matthew 10:8.)

In my personal experience, it almost seems as though miracles happen by "accident." I am certainly not thinking about miracles when amazing things suddenly seem to happen—unintentionally on my part. One time, at the close of a gathering, people had congregated at the front of the auditorium, and I just started randomly wandering among the hungry souls as I often do, laying my hands on people to pronounce the blessing of the Lord. On that day, as I was doing my typical "Holy Ghost meandering," I gently touched a lady and announced, "Miracles!" Little did I know that this lady was desperate for a major miracle. She ran out of the auditorium, found the nearest restroom, and immediately passed seven bleeding tumors. She was totally healed in a moment. It was a miracle. Reports later verified her inexplicable healing. Praise the Lord! (I wish this happened with me all the time, but maybe this is my one out of one hundred.)

Another time, when I was in New England, people had once again flocked to the front of the church sanctuary, in response to a message on Mary of Bethany called "Wasted on Jesus" that I had just completed. I had called forward those who wanted to pour out their lives on Messiah Jesus. It was not an invitation for healings and miracles; it was an appeal for people to give their all in worship and consecration to the only One who is worthy. Once again, I found myself meandering through the crowd, simply touching some, blessing them and occasionally speaking a short phase over them. Over a particular dear lady who was worshipping, I simply pronounced the word, "Healing," having no sense of anything transpiring as a result.

One year later, I was back at the very same church. The grateful woman publicly presented me with a gift of an old painting of Mary of Bethany and then shared her testimony. As I recall her words, she had come forward the year before to present herself as a "laid-down lover," and when I had gently laid my hand upon her, the fire of God had gone into her body. She had suddenly been completely healed of cancer, which, of course, I did not even know she had.

How amazing is the love of God—healings and miracles happening when the person acting as the channel of God's grace isn't even aware of what he is doing. You have to love stuff like that! As one of my next gen friends says, "You can't make stuff like that up!"

THE LEGACY OF JOHN G. LAKE

We can look to the legacy of John G. Lake (1870–1935) for inspiration on how God has used the gift of workings of miracles in the past—and what He can do in our day. Lake definitely stands out in modern church history when it comes to the power gifts of the Holy Spirit. He was a Canadian-American leader in the global Pentecostal movement and was known as a faith healer; he was also a missionary and the cofounder of the Apostolic Faith Mission in South Africa. After completing his missionary work in South Africa, Lake moved to the Northwest of the United States, where he evangelized for more than twenty years. Through his Divine Healing Institute, he set up Divine Healing Rooms in Spokane, Washington, and up and down the West Coast.

Some years ago, I was in prayer for five days at a retreat house with a mountaintop view overlooking the city of Spokane, Washington. At the end of my time of intercessory seclusion, somebody showed me a copy of a secular newspaper dated August 7, 1924, on which I read this front-page headline: "Healed by God—Parade in Streets."

The article, written by a reporter named Alan Watts, described a literal parade on the downtown streets of Spokane of two hundred fifty people who claimed to have been healed from various diseases through the ministry of John G. Lake. A permit had been granted for fifty cars and a marching band to participate in the parade. Automobiles carried signs on which were written the names of the diseases from which the occupants had been cured, such as pneumonia, diabetes, paralysis, rheumatism, shingles, eczema, nervous conditions, broken arches, and more. Lake himself had led the testimonial parade, which was appropriately followed up by a miracle service that evening at 8:00 p.m. in a tent set up at Ash and Chelan Streets.

Reading about this event made me think, *Wouldn't it be stunning to have a parade of healing like that sometime? How about a Global Day of Prayer for the Sick followed by healing and miracle gatherings held simultaneously in major cities? Do it again, God!*

THE GRAND PURPOSE OF MIRACLES

The first book that Mahesh Chavda wrote was called *Only Love Can Make a Miracle*. That title captures a profound truth. Only God, who is Love, can perform a miracle. And only by growing in His love can we participate with Him in making miracles. This is why *compassion* was such an important element in Jesus' miracles, as in this example: *"Moved with compassion, Jesus stretched out His hand and touched him [the leper], and said to him, 'I am willing; be cleansed'"* (Mark 1:41). Compassion is an expression of love, and people whom God uses to work miracles will find that compassion rises up in their hearts in response to the stirrings of the Spirit. Miracles are meant for good. God wants to protect and preserve, restore and build up. He wants to create new entry points for His kingdom of love.

Earlier, I mentioned my visiting Oral Roberts at his home in California near the end of his life. Brother Roberts was like a grandfather in the faith to all of us who were in that room. I had the honor of having my oldest son, Justin, with me on that momentous occasion, and Justin got a chance to speak to him, sitting on the ottoman at Oral's feet. "I want to move in a greater level of healings and miracles," he said.

Oral shook his head and said, "Son, you don't know what you're asking for."

But my son was persistent. Finally, Oral shifted. He stopped shaking his head and said, "Let me say this: if you want to move in healings and miracles, then you must learn to love the sick." Instead of praying for an impartation of power or a spiritual gifting, Oral just told him the big secret—"learn to love the sick." As we learn to love with Jesus' love, we become much more like Him. We get closer to Him, and we can hear His quiet words of instruction. Then, if a miracle is called for, we are ready.

God's grand purpose is to build up His kingdom. To that end, He builds up the people who populate His kingdom, and He exalts His glory through miraculous works so that more people will come to believe in Him and follow Him. From ancient times, this has been true. The miracles and plagues in Egypt had one purpose: the deliverance and preservation of the people of Israel. Again, when Jesus turned the water into wine at the wedding in Cana, it was a sign: *"What Jesus did here in Cana of Galilee was the first of the signs through which he revealed his glory; and his disciples believed in him"* (John 2:11 NIV). Subsequently, *"many other signs Jesus also performed in the presence of the disciples, which are not written in this book; but these have been written so that you may **believe** that Jesus is the Christ, the Son of God; and that **believing** you may have life in His name"* (John 20:30–31).

Miracles are meant to accompany the preaching of the gospel, working in connection with evangelism to confirm the work of the cross of Jesus and the power of the Word of God. This is the thrust of the Great Commission:

And [Jesus] said to them, "Go into all the world and preach the gospel to all creation. He who has believed and has been baptized shall be saved; but he who has disbelieved shall be condemned. These signs will accompany those who have believed: in My name they will cast out demons, they will speak with new tongues; they will pick up serpents, and if they drink any deadly poison, it will not hurt them; they will lay hands on the sick, and they will recover." So then, when the Lord Jesus had spoken to them, He was received up into heaven and sat down at the right hand of God. And they went out and preached everywhere, while the Lord worked with them, and confirmed the word by the signs that followed. (Mark 16:15–20)

Jesus has made us co-laborers with Him by the miracle-working power of His Holy Spirit. He does not hoard all of the excitement; to this day, He wants His disciples to see miracles and to be the avenue of His miracle-working power in the earth. Jesus said, *"Truly, truly, I say to you, he who believes in Me, the works that I do, he will do also; and greater works than these he will do; because I go to the Father. Whatever you ask in My name, that will I do, so that the Father may be glorified in the Son"* (John 14:12–13), and, *"All things are possible to him who believes"* (Mark 9:23).

May Your kingdom come, Lord! Where miracles are concerned, we haven't seen anything yet, compared with the glory yet to be revealed! Do it again in our lives, Holy Spirit—today!

Father, I give You thanks and declare that You are good all the time. Because it is Your nature to be loving and extravagant, I know that You have made the gifts of the Holy Spirit freely available to me and to every believer, through Your Son Christ Jesus. I welcome the gift of workings of miracles into every sphere of my life, and I look with expectation to see You release demonstrations of Your glory in the church and in the society around me. I go forward anticipating that something good, powerful, and supernatural is poised to happen! Amen.

SECTION FOUR

VOCAL GIFTS—THE GIFTS THAT SPEAK

The final set of gifts focuses on the gifts that articulate God's thought. In chapter 10, we begin with the gift of various kinds of tongues. I explain that the gift of tongues for personal communication with God is given to all believers, regardless of their educational background. Without their having cracked a foreign language book or lived in a foreign country, the Holy Spirit enables them to begin to speak in another language (tongue). Although they can't understand what they're speaking, they speak expressively, fluently, and smoothly.

In this chapter, I also address important issues related to the gift of various kinds of tongues, including why the Spirit chooses to bestow the gift of tongues on any believer who wants it, why we should speak in tongues, and specific guidelines for using tongues in a group setting to prevent misuse of the gift.

In chapter 11, we move to the gift of interpretation of tongues. The purpose of this gift is to make what was spoken in tongues—in the context of an assembly of believers—intelligible to the hearers (and to the one who spoke out in tongues) in their vernacular so that everyone might be edified, or built up. As with the gift of tongues, the gift of interpretation of tongues has absolutely nothing to do with a natural knowledge of languages; the comprehension comes directly from the Holy Spirit. Similar to the previous chapter, I provide some basic guidelines for using the gift of interpretation of tongues in a gathering of believers.

In chapter 12, we conclude our examination of the gifts of the Spirit with the gift of prophecy. I start this chapter with a key point that is especially relevant for the times in which we live: people who have been given the gift of prophecy do not necessarily predict future events. In fact, most of the time, they don't. A prophecy is a brief, supernatural word of hope and encouragement, often personalized and always in alignment with the truth of Scripture. It has three main purposes: to edify, to exhort, and to comfort.

In this final chapter, I give a glimpse of the gift of prophecy as it functioned in the New Testament church. Seeing how the gift was implemented in the early church gives us insights into its purpose and use and how we can grow in our own use of it. Finally, I list a variety of ways that the prophetic word can be released or expressed to accomplish its purpose. The ultimate purpose of prophecy is to release the testimony of Jesus.

10

THE GIFT OF VARIOUS KINDS OF TONGUES

"Men of Judea and all you who live in Jerusalem, let this be known to you and give heed to my words. For these men are not drunk, as you suppose, for it is only the third hour of the day; but this is what was spoken of through the prophet Joel: 'And it shall be in the last days,' God says, 'that I will pour forth of My Spirit on all mankind....'"
—Acts 2:14–17

If you undertake a thorough investigation of church history, you will find that the spiritual gifts have never fully ceased, although they have ebbed at times; and as I wrote earlier, they have been disparaged by Christians who believed that the gifts ceased after the first generation of apostles died. Repeatedly, interest in the gifts has come in waves, and the waves and their ripples have affected some parts of the church more than others.

Currently, we are surfing a big wave that gathered strength around 1900 with the outpouring of the Holy Spirit at a humble place on Azusa Street in Southern California and has resulted in whole new "categories" of Christians—Pentecostals (named after the Acts 2 outpouring of the Spirit on the day of Pentecost) and charismatics (named after the *charismata*, or spiritual gifts). Although we still have sincere, cessationist believers who assert that the spiritual gifts passed away at the completion and establishment of the canon of Scripture, church growth is exploding wherever the gifts of the Holy Spirit are on display. These vital gifts act as fuel to the fire of church growth.

Questions about spiritual gifts can no longer be answered in an academic manner when people see the fruitful flourishing of many branches of the body of Christ, all blossoming with the brilliance of the manifest presence of God. Many believers in mainline denominations worldwide consider themselves to be "Bapticostals" or "Methocostals" or Presbycostals" or "Luthercostals." And Pentecostalism keeps spreading rapidly, especially in the developing world, due to the targeted missionary efforts of these denominations. When you add in the emerging, twenty-first-century New Apostolic Reformation global network of churches and ministries, it all adds up to a wholesale explosion! I am a part of an apostolic team called Harvest International Ministries, which, in less than twenty years, has grown to include over twenty-five thousand new churches in its international network. This is just a glimpse of what the Holy Spirit is doing in our day!

The Pentecostal, charismatic, third-wave, and New Apostolic Reformation movements have been used over the past one-hundred-plus years to restore the gift of tongues in an amazing manner worldwide. Some of the other gifts, such as healings, miracles, or prophecy, may appear in certain periods to have eclipsed the emphasis on the gift of tongues. But due to the scriptural, foundational teaching on the baptism of the Holy Spirit, the gift of tongues will just not take a back seat; it comes with the full gifts package. Although times and seasons might highlight first one gift and then another, that does not change the fact that each and every one of the spiritual gifts is valid and active today.

"TONGUES"—WHAT'S THAT?

I imagine that many of the readers of this book will already know about the gift of tongues, usually from firsthand experience, because tongues is a gift for every believer in Christ Jesus. Just as every believer is meant to be filled with the Holy Spirit, so every believer has the option of praying or speaking in tongues. Some people argue that speaking in tongues is the initial and only true proof of being baptized in the Spirit. I do not go that far, but I would say that it is an eventual evidence—and very good evidence, for sure!

The gift of tongues is definitely miraculous. It is given to people regardless of their educational background; some people who exercise the gift may not even have learned to read or write. Without their having cracked a foreign language book or lived in a foreign country, the Holy Spirit enables them to begin to speak in another language (tongue)—and they can continue to speak in this language, by an act of their will, at their choosing. They can't understand what they're speaking, but they can speak expressively, fluently, and smoothly. Their particular tongue may be identifiable as a known language—one of the *tongues of men*" (1 Corinthians 13:1)— and on occasion they may be understood by a native speaker. Or it may be a heavenly language—one of the *tongues…of angels*" (1 Corinthians 13:1). Almost never is a person's God-given tongue a language that the person has learned to speak, even in part. As Kenneth Hagin wrote, "Speaking with tongues has nothing whatsoever to do with linguistic ability….It is a vocal miracle of the Holy Spirit."[1]

Normally, those of us who speak in tongues reserve the gift for use in our private devotions, but some might speak out by the Spirit's prompting in live worship settings or, very occasionally, in a public, secular situation. Once in a while, the Spirit inspires someone to speak temporarily in an entirely different tongue from their usual one in order to communicate with another party. Once, I spoke out in Greek, and it was understood by others; I have never done this since, that I know of. I have also been known to speak in Russian and Korean, as well as in K'iche', a language used by the indigenous inhabitants of the Guatemalan highlands. (I will tell you that story in the next chapter!)

Some of the New Testament references to tongues relate to the public use of the gift, while others relate only to its private, devotional use. (This does not imply that two different gifts are involved, however. Any person who speaks publicly in tongues also uses the gift in private.[2]) Besides using the gift in private devotions, people also pray Spirit-inspired intercessory prayers by using the gift of tongues. That is how most of us interpret the following Scripture passage:

> *Likewise the Spirit helps us in our weakness; for we do not know how to pray as we ought, but that very Spirit intercedes with sighs* [many other translations use *"groans"* or *"groanings"*] *too deep for words. And God, who searches the heart, knows what is the mind of the Spirit, because the Spirit intercedes for the saints according to the will of God.* (Romans 8:26–27 NRSV)

The *"sighs"* or *"groanings"* might refer to tongues, but they might also refer to something beyond tongues, because a person who prays in this way is too overwhelmed for words. *"Sighs too deep for words"* can be like the travail of giving birth, or like Jesus weeping before the tomb of His friend Lazarus. (See John 11:32–36.) In any case, when we do not know how to pray, praying in tongues is always a viable option. When you pray in tongues, you are praying the perfect prayer, whether it is a prayer of worship or a prayer of intercession, because the Holy Spirit is praying through you!

When a person speaks in a tongue, he or she uses normal vocal organs, but the conscious mind plays no part in the operation of the gift. Yet when a person feels inspired to speak out in tongues publicly, such utterances will, ideally, be followed by an interpretation in the native language of the hearers. (Chapter 11 describes the gift of interpretation of tongues.)

Just as with the other spiritual gifts, receiving the gift of tongues is not a special sign of favor from God, nor is it a sign of superior zeal, commitment, or maturity. It is simply a manifestation of the grace of God given to believers for the common good of the church.[3] For Spirit-filled believers, speaking in tongues is an expected overflow of the infilling. (See, for example, Mark 16:17; John 7:38–39; Acts 1:8; 19:6.)

The ability to speak in tongues represents a fulfillment of the prophecy spoken by Isaiah (see Isaiah 28:11–12) and quoted by Paul in 1 Corinthians 14:21: *"In the Law it is written, 'By men of strange tongues and by the lips of strangers I will speak to this people, and even so they will not listen to Me,' says the Lord."* Although tongues were first given to the apostles and the other believers who were gathered in prayer on the day of Pentecost, that group experience alone did not fulfill the prophecy. There is an ongoing fulfillment of it. On the day of Pentecost and on other occasions, the gift of tongues proved that people had received the Holy Spirit, and to this day, the gift has continued to provide evidence that a person has received the Spirit.

The following Scriptures show how the story of the gift of tongues developed at the beginning of the early church as the scene of action shifted from Israel (Jerusalem) northwest to the Roman centurion Cornelius' house in Caesarea and across the Mediterranean Sea to Ephesus in what is now Turkey:

> *And they were all filled with the Holy Spirit and began to speak with other tongues, as the Spirit was giving them utterance. Now there were Jews living in Jerusalem, devout men from every nation under heaven. And when this sound occurred, the crowd came together, and were bewildered because each one of them was hearing them speak in his own language.* (Acts 2:4–6)

> *All the circumcised believers who came with Peter were amazed, because the gift of the Holy Spirit had been poured out on the Gentiles also. For they were hearing them speaking with tongues and exalting God. Then Peter answered, "Surely no one can refuse the water for these to be baptized who have received the Holy Spirit just as we did, can he?" And he ordered them to be baptized in the name of Jesus Christ.* (Acts 10:45–48)

> *It happened that while Apollos was at Corinth, Paul passed through the upper country and came to Ephesus, and found some disciples. He said to them, "Did you receive the Holy Spirit when you believed?" And they said to him, "No, we have not even heard whether there is a Holy*

Spirit." And he said, "Into what then were you baptized?" And they said, "Into John's baptism." Paul said, "John baptized with the baptism of repentance, telling the people to believe in Him who was coming after him, that is, in Jesus." When they heard this, they were baptized in the name of the Lord Jesus. And when Paul had laid his hands upon them, the Holy Spirit came on them, and they began speaking with tongues and prophesying. (Acts 19:1–6)

PURPOSES OF SPEAKING IN TONGUES

Why do you think the Spirit chooses to bestow the gift of tongues on any believer who wants it? I can think of a bunch of reasons, all of which we can find in Scripture.

For starters, praying and speaking in tongues represent personal communication with God—communication that is guaranteed to be on target every time, despite the limitations of our human understanding. Communication with God builds up our spirits every time. Paul explained, *"One who speaks in a tongue does not speak to men but to God…. One who speaks in a tongue edifies himself"* (1 Corinthians 14:2, 4). That is why Jude endorsed the use of the gift of tongues, which he called "praying in the Spirit": *"But you, beloved, build yourselves up on your most holy faith; pray in the Holy Spirit"* (Jude 1:20 NRSV). And Paul advised, *"Pray at all times in the Spirit"* (Ephesians 6:18). The gift of tongues can therefore be used for personal communion with God on a continual basis. Tongues is a vital gift for members of the body of Christ—like prophecy, it is useful for edification, exhortation, and comfort, especially when it is interpreted. (See 1 Corinthians 14:3–5.)

Tongues is not the only way of praying in the Holy Spirit, but it is one of the primary ways. Such prayers involve worship, of course, and they also frequently include intercession on behalf of an individual, a group of people, or a situation. Most of the time, such prayers would not require interpretation into a language that is commonly understood, although I have found myself repeating phrases in tongues to the point that I have asked the Spirit for the interpretation so I would know what I was praying for.

Intercessory prayer in tongues always hits the bull's-eye. Not long ago, in Korea, I participated in a dramatic example of this reality. I had just preached a message entitled "Rediscovering the Gift of Tongues" to several thousand Korean church leaders when someone came up to me on the platform and said, "We have received word that [a very prominent leader] has fallen into a coma." I asked all five thousand of the leaders in attendance to rise to their feet and launch an all-out prayer assault in tongues. I completely lost track of time, but someone who was there told me we prayed nonstop in a spiritual-warfare manner for thirty minutes or so. Then the atmosphere shifted, and everyone moved into exalting and praising the Lord in the gift of tongues. We could sense the shift, and we knew we had broken through together into a gift of faith. The entire assembly went into a wild exaltation of God. Very shortly after this subsided, we received word that the influential leader had aroused out of the coma during that time.

I am convinced that the Lord often uses such prayer to rebuke the forces of darkness, who can comprehend the supernatural reproofs even when the speakers do not. Surely, in such cases, the victory is often won by a combination of the prayer in tongues and the gifts of faith and discernment.

Praying in tongues is also a powerful way to express victorious praises to God, using words that are far better than what we could come up with on our own. When used for the high praises of God, this gift is a supernatural tool that will change the spiritual climate, opening the spiritual atmosphere to the power of God, which makes all things possible. That is what happened when Peter preached at Cornelius's home. During Peter's sermon, the Holy Spirit fell upon the Gentile listeners, and they began to spontaneously speak in tongues, exalting God. (See Acts 10:44–46.)

God sometimes uses the gift of tongues as a sign of His glorious presence in an assembly. This can be particularly powerful as a sign to unbelievers, and the gift has proven to be very effective on the mission field for convincing those who do not yet believe in God. *"So then tongues are for a sign, not to those who believe but to unbelievers"* (1 Corinthians 14:22). As a sign, the gift of tongues exposes unbelievers to the reality that God is alive and is personally involved in His people's lives. Also, utterances in unknown tongues signify that the resurrection of Jesus Christ really happened—that He is risen and glorified. Peter said to the awed unbelievers on the day of

Pentecost, *"Therefore having been exalted to the right hand of God, and having received from the Father the promise of the Holy Spirit, [Jesus] has poured forth this which you both see and hear"* (Acts 2:33). The gift of tongues was a powerful sign to observers on the day of Pentecost who knew for a fact that none of those uneducated Galileans could possibly have learned so many foreign languages. (See Acts 2:7–11.) As we see from that first episode of mass tongues-speaking, such supernatural occurrences can result in amazingly successful evangelism. (See Acts 2:41, 47.)

So you see that while speaking in tongues may be considered one of the initial manifestations of being filled with the Holy Spirit (like an overflow of the infilling), it is more than that. The gift of tongues is a means of *staying* filled with the Spirit continuously. As I mentioned in chapter 2, we all "leak." Each one of us remains a work in progress. We carry around the dust of the earth, and we have wounds and cracks. In addition, on behalf of others, we may pour out what we can contain of the Spirit, and then we need to be replenished. Take it from me, speaking and praying in tongues is not the only way to be refilled with the Spirit when your well runs dry, but it is an easily-accessed way of "priming the pump." What a wonderful, multipurpose gift!

WHY SHOULD I SPEAK IN TONGUES?

Accepting the gift of tongues is an acknowledgment of one's personal acceptance of Jesus' lordship, in that it requires total yieldedness even of our most *"unruly"* member, the tongue. (See James 3:3–12 NKJV, KJV). Since the day of Pentecost, speaking in tongues has proved to be a sign of repentance and of reception of the Spirit:

> Now when they heard this [the message of salvation], *they were pierced to the heart, and said to Peter and the rest of the apostles,* "Brethren, what shall we do?" Peter said to them, "Repent, and each of you be baptized in the name of Jesus Christ for the forgiveness of your sins; and you will receive the gift of the Holy Spirit."
>
> (Acts 2:37–38; see also Acts 10:46–47)

One must become humble and childlike in order to speak to God in tongues, abandoning self-determination and self-sufficiency. (See, for example, 1 Corinthians 1:18–31; Matthew 18:2–5.) In an ongoing way, the gift of tongues succeeds in keeping pride at bay.

As we find ourselves in a receptive, childlike, and dependent position, our speaking in tongues makes it possible for God to speak to us supernaturally even as we speak to Him, and this brings edification all around. One of the most strategic ways to build up your faith is by praying in the Holy Spirit. I do it all the time, taking my cue from Paul, who wrote, *"I thank God, I speak in tongues more than you all"* (1 Corinthians 14:18).

Why should you speak in tongues? Given all of the above good reasons, why should you *not* speak in tongues? It is one of God's best gifts, and the fact that He is so generous with it proves how important it is. Sometimes, people start to think that tongues is just a commonplace spiritual gift, and therefore of lesser importance. However, the reason the gift of tongues is not the least of the gifts is that it is like an on-ramp to the highway of the other gifts. The more you pray in tongues, the more you will be able to tell what the Spirit of God is doing and how He may want you to participate with Him in it.

I mentioned in chapter 2 how the Lord once told me that if I prayed in tongues for two hours in one sitting, He would give me a spirit of revelation. At first, I found it difficult to stick to praying in tongues for that long. Then the Lord helped me to see that because I was a singer before I was ever a preacher, I could sing and worship in tongues and do it for lengthy periods of time without tiring of it. I found that I could pray and sing or worship in tongues for hours on end. Revelation flowed as a result; and through my ministry, I was able to richly bless many people. For me, worshipping and praying in the gift of tongues is honestly not a lot of work—it is an absolute delight!

I am not able to follow this practice as consistently today because of my travels, my writing, and my additional responsibilities, such as equipping other believers to use their spiritual gifts. But it is still a practice that I highly value, and when God indicates that He wants me to worship and pray in tongues for hours a day, I jump right back into it. It is an honor to do so, and it is an effective tool of the Holy Spirit!

GUIDELINES FOR SPEAKING IN TONGUES

In 1 Corinthians, Paul wrote very explicit guidelines for speaking in tongues, both in private and in public church meetings, and his advice is not meant only for the church in Corinth to which he addressed that letter. He acknowledged that not everyone who exercises a tongue in private communion with God will also exercise the public ministry of tongues. (See 1 Corinthians 12:29–30.) He also indicated that in a public assembly, it is out of place to speak out loud in a tongue without being prompted by God's special leading and without supplying the interpretation:

> *I thank God, I speak in tongues more than you all; however, in the church I desire to speak five words with my mind so that I may instruct others also, rather than ten thousand words in a tongue.... If anyone speaks in a tongue, it should be by two or at the most three, and each in turn, and one must interpret; but if there is no interpreter, he must keep silent in the church; and let him speak to himself and to God.*
> (1 Corinthians 14:18–19, 27–28)

In other words, it is perfectly okay to pray in tongues to yourself in a church setting; that is not forbidden at all. In fact, it is encouraged! But unrestrained tongues-speaking can be out of place when exercised in the wrong setting. Public utterances in tongues should occur within the guidelines of the fruit of the Spirit (see Galatians 5:22–23), and they should be interpreted into a commonly understood language. An intercessory prayer gathering, however, is an appropriate place to engage in corporate, even loud, praying in the Spirit. As I shared in the story from Korea, it brings results, and we should never limit God!

As previously mentioned, I also believe that there are appropriate times for corporate *singing* in tongues, or singing in the Spirit, when a group of people segue from using their ordinary language for worshipping in prayer and song to singing in tongues corporately, harmonizing in the Spirit. Sometimes it happens that this involves interpretation, anyway, as one person sings in the Spirit and another person sings the interpretation. But when a whole group of people sings together in the Spirit, most of the "lyrics" will be in uninterpreted tongues, which creates an amazing atmosphere of pure worship. Numerous times, I have been present in a meeting when this form of corporate worship has resulted in a "glory realm" of the Lord descending upon His people. A little bit of heaven descends to earth—and there ain't nothing like it! So join me today and sing in the Spirit!

Guidelines for speaking in tongues, therefore, will always depend on the situation. We should respect the protocol of the particular house of worship. "*Do not forbid speaking in tongues,*" Paul wrote, "*but all things should be done decently and in order*" (1 Corinthians 14:39–40 NRSV). "*Decently and in order*" means different things in different places. In many Pentecostal and charismatic churches, if the people sense that the Holy Spirit is moving, worshipful tongues-speaking will burst out across the room, and no one will be offended. It is never wrong to follow Paul's instruction to "*follow the way of love and eagerly desire gifts of the Spirit*" (1 Corinthians 14:1 NIV). Following the way of love means sticking close to the Spirit of Christ Jesus, who will help us navigate through storms, equipping us with the very words we need for each stage of the journey.

Lord, I am hungry and thirsty for more of You! Give me a fresh baptism of the Holy Spirit and stir up in me the gift of praying, worshipping, and speaking in tongues. I want everything You have for me. I want to build myself up in my most holy faith. Please release all the gifts of the Holy Spirit in my life and in the lives of my family members. Send the Spirit now more powerfully into my church, my city, and my region, for Jesus Christ's sake. Amen.

11

THE GIFT OF INTERPRETATION
OF TONGUES

"One who speaks in a tongue should pray for the power to interpret."
—1 Corinthians 14:13 (NRSV)

anifestations of the other seven primary gifts of the Spirit appeared in the Old Testament, but the gifts of tongues and interpretation of tongues do not seem to be mentioned by earlier writers except to be prophesied about. As I noted in the previous chapter, Paul made the connection when he quoted from Isaiah 28:11–12 in his instruction about tongues to the church in Corinth in 1 Corinthians 14:21. The gift of the interpretation of tongues is therefore distinct to Christianity since the day of Pentecost, alongside the gift of tongues.

This gift bears a special relationship to the baptism of the Holy Spirit, which first took place at Pentecost. On that occasion, many of the tongues that were spoken aloud simultaneously by the disciples were understood immediately by the listeners who gathered in the street. Jerusalem was crowded with visitors from many other nations, and Luke's account in Acts tells us that all of them heard the good news being proclaimed in their own tongues. As if that were not enough of a miracle, Peter went on to preach in the language that most of them had in common, providing essentially a more complete interpretation or understanding of the messages of proclamation that had been spoken in tongues.

THE GIFT OF INTERPRETATION OF TONGUES DEFINED

Derek Prince wrote, "Interpretation must not necessarily be understood to mean a word-for-word translation, but rather a rendering of the general sense of what was spoken in the tongue."[1] John Wimber and others have called this a "dynamic equivalent."[2] The purpose of the gift is to make what was spoken in tongues intelligible to the hearers (and to the one who spoke out in tongues) in their vernacular so that everyone might be edified or built up.[3] Obviously, the operation of the gift depends not only on the Holy Spirit but also on a person's action of speaking in tongues immediately prior to the interpretation.[4] As with the gift of tongues, the gift of interpretation of tongues "has absolutely nothing to do with natural linguistic ability"; the comprehension comes directly from the Holy Spirit.[5]

With Sam Storms, I am convinced that the gift of interpretation of tongues may be the most overlooked of the primary gifts of the Holy Spirit.[6] We have not begun to tap into the power of this gift, and we need to! If nothing else, it enables us to understand what we're praying or singing in the Spirit, but it is even more valuable than that. Paul wrote, "*I will pray with the spirit and I will pray with the mind also; I will sing with the spirit and I will sing with the mind also*" (1 Corinthians 14:15). We need more of this today, both in corporate worship settings and in our private devotions. I am talking about something more than what we're used to in our gatherings where tongues and interpretation occur. When someone speaks a message in a tongue and then, after a gap of maybe fifteen seconds, somebody speaks out the interpretation, that is valid enough; but it is only one application of the gift of interpretation of tongues. Keeping ourselves to that one application seems to limit the free moving of the Holy Spirit.

The late Oral Roberts used to take people on tours of Oral Roberts University, and he would say, "You see all of this? All of this was built by praying in tongues." He got the vision for every building by praying in tongues and then interpreting his own tongues back to himself. In fact, he recommended that people learn to do that by praying in tongues for five minutes, and then stopping and speaking in their native language, which he taught would either be an interpretation of the mystery the person had just uttered in tongues or a prophetic prayer, both of which would be beneficial to the quality of the prayer.

While this gift may be somewhat neglected today, Paul did not neglect it, just as he did not neglect the gift of tongues. In fact, he listed these two gifts and discussed them much more often than he did many of the other gifts. Above all, he urged everyone to employ the gifts of the Spirit by means of the love of God. (See 1 Corinthians 13.) He wanted love to be our aim in everything we do. How about you?

GUIDELINES FOR INTERPRETATION OF TONGUES

The gift of interpretation of tongues operates differently through different believers. It has *"diversities of operations,"* as the King James Version translates Paul's words in 1 Corinthians 12:6: *"There are diversities of operations, but it is the same God which worketh all in all."* For some people, an interpretation comes to mind as just one introductory phrase, and they must "launch out in faith" before they receive the rest, while others hear words and whole sentences in their minds, or see words displayed on a scroll or a screen in their mind's eye. Still others receive visions that they go on to relate in their own words; or, a general thought may drop into their minds, which they "clothe with words of their own choosing," as the Holy Spirit leads them. Every mode of operation depends on faith to a significant degree. If you sit tight waiting for a complete message to be dropped into your head, you will just sit there until it is too late, because that is not the way it works.[7]

A message of exhortation that comes by tongues and interpretation is the same as a prophecy, and it should be judged by the same standards. (Kenneth Hagin used to say that if prophecy is like a dime, then tongues plus interpretation can often be like two nickels.) However, this equivalent of prophecy, which can be called an "exhorting tongue," or a "message tongue," is not the same as a "mystery tongue" used for personal devotions. Paul drew this contrast when he wrote,

> For one who speaks in a tongue does not speak to men but to God; for no one understands, but in his spirit he speaks mysteries. But one who prophesies speaks to men for edification and exhortation and consolation. One who speaks in a tongue edifies himself; but one who prophesies edifies the church. (1 Corinthians 14:2–4)

Paul's guidelines for using tongues and interpretation in church gatherings apply to exhorting tongues or message tongues only, not to the personal use of the gift, in which the meaning of the words often remains a mystery. (See 1 Corinthians 14:26–32.[8])

Now, a message in tongues and its interpretation do not necessarily need to come from two different people. If necessary, the person who delivers the message in tongues can pray to receive an interpretation and go ahead and speak it aloud, whether in an appropriate public assembly or privately. In some ministries, this practice is not encouraged, but I believe we should make room for every gift and operation of the Holy Spirit, embracing them rather than shunning them. Don't box God up! If you do, He might just burst right out!

In meetings that are geared toward evangelism, which one would expect to be attended by unbelievers, I can understand keeping those gifts out of sight a little more. But from my perspective, this is not the case in gatherings that are meant mostly for worshipping believers. I think the final guidelines should come from the leaders of each gathering. Read Paul's advice below, keeping in mind the contrast between uninterpreted devotional tongues used in a worship setting as compared to interpreted exhorting tongues, or message tongues:

So then tongues are for a sign, not to those who believe but to unbelievers; but prophecy is for a sign, not to unbelievers but to those who believe. Therefore if the whole church assembles together and all speak in tongues, and ungifted men or unbelievers enter, will they not say that you are mad? But if all prophesy, and an unbeliever or an ungifted man enters, he is convicted by all, he is called to account by all; the secrets of his heart are disclosed; and so he will fall on his face and worship God, declaring that God is certainly among you. (1 Corinthians 14:22–25)

Just to be clear, I am not at all precluding the interpretation of devotional tongues. As a matter of fact, a person who is praying mysteries to God in tongues might find it very upbuilding to hear an interpretation of the prayer he or she just prayed, whether the prayer was high praises of God or spiritual warfare. I have been in meetings in which tongues and interpretation come off almost like a conversation. (This works especially well in leadership gatherings or smaller groups, such as home groups.) One speaks in tongues and another interprets, going back and forth, moving around in subject matter from praises to prophecies to revelations of what has just been prayed for. You can practice this when you are by yourself until you feel freer in it. I would do in public only what I have practiced in private. Remember, though, spiritual gifts are tools, not toys!

DIVERSITIES OF TONGUES, DIVERSITIES OF INTERPRETATIONS

Now there are varieties of gifts, but the same Spirit. And there are varieties of ministries, and the same Lord. There are varieties of effects, but the same God who works all things in all persons. But to each one is given the manifestation of the Spirit for the common good. For to one [and to another are given various gifts, including]...*various kinds of tongues, and to another the interpretation of tongues. But one and the same Spirit works all these things, distributing to each one individually just as He wills.*

(1 Corinthians 12:4–8, 10–11; see also Romans 12:3–8)

The key idea is diversity—an endless variety of languages and a limitless array of interpretations—as appointed and inspired by the Holy Spirit. Again, in public situations, people do not speak out in tongues or interpretations whenever they wish, but only as they are led by the Spirit to do so. The orchestration is up to God.

Boundaries are important. That is why Paul wrote these instructions: "*If anyone speaks in a tongue, it should be by two or at the most three, and each in turn, and one must interpret; but if there is no interpreter, he must keep silent in the church; and let him speak to himself and to God*" (1 Corinthians 14:27–28). In a church setting, two or three messages are usually sufficient for the assembly to understand clearly the gist of what the Lord is saying. (Again, this advice applies only to the public use of the gift of tongues and interpretation, not to private devotional use.) If a few people are involved in bringing the message, extra nuances of God's words can be received and appreciated, and no one person can claim the limelight.

Since there are always more tongues-speakers than there are people who can interpret a message in tongues, we have been invited to pray for this gift of interpretation: "*Therefore, one who speaks in a tongue should pray for the power to interpret*" (1 Corinthians 14:13 NRSV). Remember, it is a gift given by God, not something that a person can study for as you might do in order to learn a foreign language. Interpretation of tongues is very much like the gift of prophecy, for which we are also invited to ask: "*Pursue love, yet desire earnestly spiritual gifts, but especially that you may prophesy*" (1 Corinthians 14:1).

Do remember, as well, that interpretation is not the same as word-for-word translation. If the message was sung, for instance, the interpretation may or may not be sung, too, and the tune may well be different. Because I was a singer before I was a preacher, I will often launch out in singing in the Spirit to get the congregation engaged on a higher level of participation, as they sing in the Spirit also. This helps to create an atmosphere of revelation in which I might end up interpreting the corporate song that has just been sung. Believe me, it is amazing!

The interpretation is often longer or shorter than the message released in tongues. The best scriptural example of this is Daniel's interpretation of the mysterious words *"Menē, menē, tekēl, upharsin"*—his interpretation was about nine times as long as the original message. (See Daniel 5:24–28.) Sometimes people suspect that an interpretation is incorrect because the message in tongues was three minutes long and the interpretation took about fifteen seconds to deliver. But just think: The message in tongues might have repeated the same thing three times, and the interpretation could have simply summed it up. Or perhaps the tongues happened to be a "wordy" language and the message in tongues would not require as many syllables to be interpreted in the native language. Because languages sometimes differ from each other significantly, the time required to convey the essence of a message can vary greatly from one language to another. There is so much diversity within the gifts of tongues and interpretation that only God can account for all the possibilities!

THE GIFT OF INTERPRETING KNOWN LANGUAGES WITHOUT LEARNING THEM

There is a lady in Kansas City who has been given the supernatural ability to interpret known languages without learning them. She was once part of a group hosting a Spirit-filled Catholic priest from Italy. They hadn't arranged to have an interpreter, so when he started speaking, she interpreted what he said. After that, she ended up visiting his group of Franciscans in Italy, and she was able to read and translate from some ancient document that was written in early Italian, the same kind of Italian dialect that St. Francis of Assisi spoke. She had never even heard it before. The Franciscan friars could understand her perfectly—she was calling them back to their origins.

One time, I was ministering in Guatemala City, speaking at a gathering of leaders, and I just felt that we were supposed to pray in tongues out loud together for fifteen minutes. So we started doing this, and because I was up front, I was praying into the microphone. Suddenly, Harold Caballeros, the main apostolic leader of the group, stopped me. "Do you know what you're saying?" he asked in English. Harold knows quite a few languages.

"Well," I hesitated. "I'm speaking in tongues."

Harold held up two fingers. "You're speaking two different languages," he said. "First of all, you're speaking Korean. Second, you're speaking K'iche', the native language of the people of the Central American hill tribes." (That language name sounded like the word *quiche* to me; I had never heard of it before.)

That was amazing, of course, but let me tell you what happened next. We all went off to the World Congress on Evangelism, held at a convention center in Guatemala City. I was speaking at the podium when an anointing came upon me to speak in tongues. Almost immediately, about a hundred short men and women came running to the front, all dressed in clothing made from the same print of fabric, which identified them as coming from the same village. Apparently, I was speaking in K'iche' again, and evidently I had summoned them to come forward. In this case, it was not necessary for the tongues message to be interpreted, because these men and women who spoke K'iche' could understand every word. The Holy Spirit came upon them as a group, and they were overwhelmed by His glorious power.

BE SENSITIVE TO THE SPIRIT

No interpretation of tongues was needed in the examples above. No interpretation was needed on the day of Pentecost, either, because the people could easily understand the messages spoken in their own native languages. But for situations where interpretation is needed, it is good to be ready. And the only way we can be ready is to grow in our experience of responding to the Holy Spirit, which builds our confidence along with building our "spiritual muscles."

Ask the Spirit to build on your gift of tongues by granting you a gift of interpretation of tongues. Stir up the gift and learn something new from each occasion. The Lord will often move strongly and clearly when you are a beginner; and then, as you learn to be sensitive to His signals, and your confidence grows, the intensity will subside.

You do not need to concern yourself with interpretation when you are speaking in your personal "mystery tongue" in your times alone with God. In those times, it is perfectly right to get lost in God and to pray and sing in the Spirit (although it is never "illegal" to get an interpretation of your own tongues). But do try to grow in your sensitivity to God's voice for those times when a public message in tongues requires an interpretation.

A TESTIMONY OF IMPARTATION

Recently, I had just completed some physical therapy and was on my way to go grocery shopping for my oldest daughter's birthday party. She wanted chocolate cheesecake, and I knew where to find the best chocolate cheesecake, but as I was pulling out of the physical therapy parking lot, the name of a different grocery store popped into my mind. I thought to myself, *That does not make any sense…. That is not the right store.* But the name kept coming to me like the persistent word of knowledge that it was. So off I headed to the store that I knew would not have what I wanted to buy.

When I arrived and walked through the sliding glass doors, right there stood a young mother with two children, just beaming at me. She slowly approached me and asked if I might be James Goll. I responded a little humorously, "Sometimes." She lit up like a Christmas tree and started talking a mile a minute. Her two little kids were very intently watching their sweet mom as she got more and more energized.

She proceeded to tell me that she was very hungry for more of the Lord and that she had surfed the Internet at midnight the night before searching for something that would help her. She also told me that she belonged to a church that teaches that the gifts of the Holy Spirit, and especially the gift of tongues, are "of the devil." I smiled as I listened.

She exclaimed, "Then I watched this TV show last night where some lady named Patricia King and some man named James Goll were talking about the power of speaking in tongues. I told the Lord, 'If this is of You, I want it!'" She was immediately baptized in the Holy Spirit and started speaking in tongues. She kept speaking in tongues until 3:00 a.m.!

I proceeded to tell her more: "Now, when you first started speaking, it was in something like French. Is that right? And then later it shifted to some Asian language. Right? And then a warrior anointing came upon you, and you started interceding in the gift of tongues for your family. Is that right?" She was so excited. I had confirmed and interpreted her experience for her. We were about to have a revival meeting right there in the middle of the aisle at the grocery store!

"Yes, how do you know?" she asked.

"Oh, I just know these things sometimes," I replied.

She went on to tell me that after three hours of this, she had cried out to the Lord and said, "Lord, if this is of You, let me meet that crazy man James Goll today."

"Well, here I am," I affirmed. "And the Holy Spirit directed me to come here. By the way, do you know where I can buy some cheesecake?" I did get what I had come for, and she received a confirmation that her experience was authentic.

A few weeks later, I was ministering at a vibrant, new Spirit-filled church in my local area, and I was doing a book signing at the closing. This same woman surprised me by coming up to the table all excited. She told me that she now attended that very church!

Ha! I was just looking for cheesecake. She was looking for "More, Lord!"

NOW USE YOUR GIFT

Is it your turn to exercise the gift of interpretation of tongues? Are you "getting something"? Practice at home. Practice while doing your laundry or cleaning your car. Practice as you go on prayer walks in your neighborhood. First, pray in the Spirit and sing in the Spirit. Then shift from the gift of tongues into the gift of interpretation of tongues. Pray and sing with your understanding. Mysteries will be revealed. Prayers will be understood. Revelation will come. Evangelism may occur.

Miracles are just waiting to break out as you learn to move back and forth from the natural to the supernatural, and from the supernatural to the natural!

Lord, I am grateful that You are pouring out the gifts of Your Holy Spirit all across the globe. I declare that I am hungry and thirsty for more of You. Guide me into the ways of praying in the gift of tongues and of interpreting my prayers with clear understanding. Release new levels of power. Release through me fresh expressions of being led by Your Spirit, with Your fruit and Your gifts equally blended. I choose to let love be my aim, and I earnestly desire Your spiritual gifts. Thank You, Lord, that I live in such a time as this! Amen.

12

THE GIFT OF PROPHECY

*"No prophecy ever came by human will, but men and women moved
by the Holy Spirit spoke from God."*
—2 Peter 1:21 (NRSV)

It may surprise you to know that people who have been given the gift of prophecy do not necessarily predict future events. In fact, most of the time, they don't. And most of us who prophesy have never considered wearing a John-the-Baptist-style hair shirt! Despite popular depictions of prophets as solitary wilderness-dwellers, today's prophets are ordinary members of the body of Christ who have the ability to present a straightforward "human report of a divine revelation."[1]

THE GIFT OF PROPHECY DEFINED

As Derek Prince has said, prophets are those who have learned to possess and cultivate a "supernaturally imparted ability to hear the voice of the

Holy Spirit and speak God's mind and counsel...not only to the assembled group of believers, but also to individuals." What is a typical prophetic message like? Spoken in a normal tone of voice, prophecies are brief, supernatural words of hope and encouragement, often personalized and always in alignment with the truth of Scripture. They have three main purposes: (1) to *edify*, or build up, the hearers in order to strengthen them in their faith and to make them more effective in their outreach to others; (2) to *exhort* or encourage (which can include admonishment and motivation); and (3) to *comfort*, or "cheer up," those to whom the word is released. Thus we can see that prophecy is invaluable as a means of overcoming "two of Satan's greatest and most frequently used weapons against God's people... condemnation and discouragement."[2]

Prophecies are spoken in the everyday language of the prophet and the hearers, rather than in unknown tongues. In the New Testament, the Greek verb for *prophesy, propheteia*, "signifies 'the speaking forth of the mind and counsel of God.'"[3] Prophecy puts the intents and purposes of God's mind into words that everybody can understand. In the Old Testament, the Hebrew root word often translated as the verb *prophesy* is *nābâ'*, meaning to "speak (or sing) by inspiration (in prediction or simple discourse)."[4] Even as they come forth, prophetic utterances remain under the control of the speaker, whose own mind and will are fully engaged; they do not burst forth spontaneously.

As with the other gifts, the gift of prophecy should never be considered a skill, an aptitude, or a talent. It is a supernatural endowment. Prophets speak forth words that the Spirit has given them for a particular situation, and they stop speaking when the words run out. I should note that prophecy is not limited to prose sentences; sometimes prophecies come in the form of poetry (think of many Old Testament prophets), and sometimes they come with an accompanying tune, as a song.[5]

PROPHECY IN THE NEW TESTAMENT

The gift of prophecy appears in all of the scriptural listings of spiritual gifts (see 1 Corinthians 12:10, 28; Ephesians 4:11; Romans 12:6), and prophets/prophetesses are mentioned multiple times throughout the

New Testament (see Luke 2:36; 7:24–28; Acts 11:27–28; 15:32; 21:9–11). The priest Zacharias, the father of John the Baptist, *"was filled with the Holy Spirit, and prophesied"* (Luke 1:67) about his baby son, announcing that he would grow up to become a prophet: *"And you, child, will be called the prophet of the Most High; for you will go on before the Lord to prepare His ways"* (Luke 1:76; see verses 67–80 for Zacharias's entire prophecy). The One whose ways John prepared, and whom he announced, was the long-awaited Messiah, Jesus, whose life and death fulfilled so many Old Testament prophecies that entire books have been devoted to the theme.

After Jesus was resurrected and ascended to heaven, and after His Spirit was bestowed on His disciples, prophecies played an important role in the ongoing development of the body of believers He had left behind to do His work. The leaders of the early church relied heavily on both prayer and prophecy as they directed the growth of the young church. Many of them could prophesy, but the names of the particular prophets are not often recorded. For example, when a prophetic word selected Barnabas and Saul for special assignments, gospel writer Luke simply reported that *"the Holy Spirit said,"* not the name of the prophet through whom He said it: *"While they were ministering to the Lord and fasting, the Holy Spirit said, 'Set apart for Me Barnabas and Saul for the work to which I have called them'"* (Acts 13:2). The prophetic word they received for Saul and Barnabas was directive; it told them what to do and how to do it.

Later, prophecies revealed Timothy's appointed ministry, and they strengthened him in spiritual warfare as he fulfilled that ministry. We see this from Paul's first letter to Timothy:

> *Timothy, my son, I am giving you this command in keeping with the prophecies once made about you, so that by recalling them you may fight the battle well, holding on to faith and a good conscience.*
> (1 Timothy 1:18–19 NIV)

By bringing to mind the prophetic words of the Lord, Timothy could pick up *"the sword of the Spirit, which is the word of God"* (Ephesians 6:17), which is such an important part of a spiritual warrior's armor. The word of God that is called the sword of the Spirit is not, as many people assume, the written Word of God, but rather the spoken, revelatory, *rhema* word. That is the Greek word that is used in Ephesians. Timothy had been equipped for his ministry when the group of elders laid hands on him and prayed—at which time a gift from God was imparted to him by means of a prophetic word. Paul referred to this fact when he wrote to Timothy, *"Do not neglect the spiritual gift within you, which was bestowed on you through prophetic utterance with the laying on of hands by the presbytery"* (1 Timothy 4:14).

As Paul's life and ministry continued, we see personal prophetic words of direction being given to him again and again. What happened toward the end of his life is instructive: Paul himself must have been hearing the specific nuances of God's prophetic message better than the seasoned, recognized prophets around him. All of them were hearing that Paul would be persecuted if he went to Jerusalem. (See Acts 20:22–23.) Agabus and apparently the four prophetess daughters of the evangelist Philip, along with many others, were warning him against continuing on his way to Jerusalem. (See Acts 21:4, 8–11.) Agabus even acted out his prophetic warning:

> A prophet named Agabus came down from Judea. And coming to us, he took Paul's belt and bound his own feet and hands, and said, "This is what the Holy Spirit says: 'In this way the Jews at Jerusalem will bind the man who owns this belt and deliver him into the hands of the Gentiles.'"
> (Acts 21:10–11)

Yet Paul himself was undeterred. He listened carefully to what the others were saying, but he made his assessment on the basis of what the Holy Spirit was saying to him personally. The Spirit was probably reassuring him that he would be strengthened in the midst of the persecutions, and that he did not need to be afraid in the face of the upcoming hardships. The prophets recognized that, as accurate as their words were, that did not mean that the prophets had the whole picture, and the prophets respected Paul's decision. They did not violate Paul's will or force their advice on him. Admirably, Paul took full responsibility for the consequences of his decision, which requires both personal security and maturity. Instead of praying against the persecutions or running away from them, he faced them head-on, because, we have to assume, prophetic words of reassurance were flowing through his own spirit. The people grieved because they loved Paul, but they acquiesced:

> *We* [writer Luke must be including himself] *as well as the local residents began begging him not to go up to Jerusalem. Then Paul answered, "What are you doing, weeping and breaking my heart? For I am ready not only to be bound, but even to die at Jerusalem for the name of the Lord Jesus." And since he would not be persuaded, we fell silent, remarking, "The will of the Lord be done!"* (Acts 21:12–14)

When we read the rest of the book of Acts, we find that, yes, Paul was imprisoned in Jerusalem, and this started a string of events that eventually led to his death. But we also see how completely the Spirit protected him and guided him along the way. He listened to the voice of the Spirit more than he listened to other people or to his own emotions, and he got it right.

So, we can see that the gift of prophecy was part of the modus operandi of the church from its inception, and people often received the gift of prophecy along with the gift of tongues as an evidence of the filling of the Holy Spirit. When Paul laid his hands on the believers in Ephesus, *"the Holy Spirit came on them, and they began speaking with tongues and prophesying"* (Acts 19:6). This may not happen commonly today, but it was my own personal experience. I actually began to prophesy before I was taught about prophecy, before I had ever heard of it, and well before I was ever released fully into the gift of speaking in tongues.

JUDGING AND DISCERNING PROPHECY

You cannot take most prophecy at face value, even when it seems straightforward and simple. God's bigness can never be contained in a few words spoken by a human being, and every limited human vessel is prone to errors. Paul wrote, *"For we know in part and we prophesy in part"* (1 Corinthians 13:9). And when John was an old man, he wrote, *"Beloved, do not believe every spirit, but test the spirits to see whether they are from God; because many false prophets have gone out into the world"* (1 John 4:1). All prophecies, regardless of who gives them or how important they seem, should be confirmed according to these nine scriptural tests:

1. Does the revelation edify, exhort, or console?

2. Is it in agreement with God's written Word?

3. Does it exalt Jesus Christ?

4. Does it bear good fruit? Does the character of the prophet bear good fruit?

5. If it predicts a future event, does it come to pass?

6. Does the prophetic word turn people toward God or away from Him?

7. Does it produce liberty or bondage?

8. Does it produce life, or bring death?

9. Does the Holy Spirit bear witness that it is true?[6]

We should never ignore the wisdom of testing prophetic words, especially words that "direct traffic" in some way. Derek Prince wrote,

> Paul's journey to Jerusalem was rather like going through a series of traffic lights. He came to one place after another and the light was red—stop. He stopped there and waited, the light turned green, and he went on to the next place, where the light was red. He waited, and the light turned green. And so on. We see that all through this section of Paul's life and ministry, the Spirit was bearing witness through other believers, in a combination of prophecy and other gifts, of what lay ahead.... Yet these beautiful gifts of the Spirit were actually helping and directing Paul in his ministry.[7]

Not only does testing prophetic words provide safeguards against bad decisions, but it also is part of the process of prophetic maturation. Prophets risk stepping out onto a tightrope every time they proffer a word to others, but corporate discernment provides a safety net.

PURPOSES OF THE GIFT OF PROPHECY

God is our good Father, and He wants to encourage us and to advise us. (See, for example, Hosea 6:1–3.) For each new generation, He chooses prophets to deliver fresh words to accomplish His purposes. Paul wrote about three main purposes of prophecy: *"One who prophesies speaks to men for edification and exhortation and consolation"* (1 Corinthians 14:3). As we noted earlier, *edification* refers to building up people in the faith and enabling them to be more effective in ministry. *Exhortation* pertains to admonishment and motivation for people to perform good deeds, and it is the same as encouragement. *Consolation* means giving comfort or solace, or alleviating some kind of distress.

I call prophetic encouragers "Barnie boys" and "Barnie girls" after Barnabas, a leader in the New Testament church. "Barnabas" was actually a nickname for a man named Joseph who was a Levite from the island of Cyprus. (See Acts 4:36.) *Barnabas* means "son of encouragement." Just as Barnabas built up the members of the early church, "Barnie boys" (like my friend Mickey Robinson, an international author and speaker) do the same today. Encouragement does not happen to be my prophetic bent, but I am glad to have some people like him around me! We can never have too much encouragement and upbuilding.

The gift of prophecy is also used by the Holy Spirit to convict people of sin and to convince them of God's good intentions toward them. We read the following in Paul's instruction about the use of the gift in public assemblies:

> *If an unbeliever or an inquirer comes in while everyone is prophesying, they are convicted of sin and are brought under judgment by all, as the secrets of their hearts are laid bare. So they will fall down and worship God, exclaiming, "God is really among you!"*
> (1 Corinthians 14:24–25 NIV)

Some people today wrongly teach that the use of the gift of prophecy for conviction applies only to unbelievers, as in this passage, but I think it applies to all of us, since all of us need additional convicting and convincing as we make our way toward holiness. Just as the light of God penetrates the hearts of unbelievers and inquirers, so it penetrates ours, layer by layer. It is the job of the Holy Spirit to *"convict* [or convince] *the world concerning sin and righteousness and judgment"* (John 16:8), and one of the ways the Spirit does this is by speaking His *rhema* words through prophets like you and me.

Prophecy is a revelatory gift as well as a vocal gift, and God uses it to instruct and teach us: *"For you can all prophesy in turn so that everyone may be instructed and encouraged"* (1 Corinthians 14:31 NIV). No single prophet or teacher can teach everything—it takes a "cluster anointing" to do the best job. Prophets take turns supplying pieces of wisdom and knowledge, and when they finish their day's work, God's people are stronger.

HOW TO RECEIVE PROPHETIC WORDS

People may receive prophetic words in a variety of ways, some of which are more common than others. The following are several of them.

1. Through unpremeditated utterances. Much prophecy "bubbles up" from impressions and thoughts that are spoken out or written down. Bishop Bill Hamon of Christian International is the expert here. He has probably activated more people into this form of prophecy than any individual in church history. Although I would consider some prophetic words that come after waiting on the Lord to be words of knowledge, both approaches allow the mind of Christ to emerge. (See, for example, 1 Corinthians 2:12–16.)

2. Through visions or "trances." Prophecy is not always received word for word; it often comes in visual form. Visions are mind-pictures by which God communicates using symbols or audible instructions. My "prophetic papa," Bob Jones, was a forerunner in this realm in recent church history. This man seemed to live in the "heavenlies" day and night, and visions from the Lord were his daily bread.

When God wanted the disciple named Ananias to go to Saul in Damascus, He spoke to Ananias *"in a vision."* (See Acts 9:10–16.) Other examples of prophetic visions abound, such as the awe-inspiring one that Isaiah received: *"In the year that King Uzziah died, I saw the Lord sitting on a throne, high and lifted up, and the train of His robe filled the temple"* (Isaiah 6:1 NKJV). (See also, for example, Numbers 24:1–6.)

We do not talk as much about trances as we do visions, although there is plenty of trustworthy scriptural precedent for them. A trance is a visionary state in which a person's natural consciousness and volition are suspended and transcended so that God can communicate something important. For example, when Peter was about to be told to put aside his Jewish training about what constituted "uncleanness" and go to the home of a Gentile centurion, God put him into a trance before He spoke to him in a vision:

> Peter went up on the housetop about the sixth hour to pray. But he became hungry and was desiring to eat; but while they were making preparations, he fell into a trance; and he saw the sky opened up, and an object like a great sheet coming down, lowered by four corners to the ground, and there were in it all kinds of four-footed animals and crawling creatures of the earth and birds of the air. A voice came to him, "Get up, Peter, kill and eat!" But Peter said, "By no means, Lord, for I have never eaten anything unholy and unclean." Again a voice came to him a second time, "What God has cleansed, no longer consider unholy." This happened three times, and immediately the object was taken up into the sky.   (Acts 10:9–16)

The apostle John received the entire book of Revelation while he was "in the Spirit" (i.e., in a Holy-Spirit-inspired trance) on the island called Patmos: "I was in the Spirit on the Lord's day, and I heard behind me a loud voice like the sound of a trumpet, saying, 'Write in a book what you see, and send it to the seven churches'" (Revelation 1:10–11).

3. Through dreams (night visions). I get a lot of my prophetic insight through dreams. To make it easier, I pray before I go to sleep, asking God to speak to me, and I sometimes put on a worship CD. The prophetic words I receive are not only for me, although I would say that through dreams I get a large percentage of my assignments about what to write or speak on and where. Often enough, I receive something for others so they can come to understand how much God loves them.

The Lord explained how He communicated through prophetic dreams when He spoke from the pillar of cloud to Aaron and Miriam, saying, "Hear now My words: If there is a prophet among you, I, the LORD, shall make Myself known to him in a vision. I shall speak with him in a dream" (Numbers 12:6). Here are two biblical examples of prophetic dreams that I suggest you look up: Daniel 7:1–28 ("Daniel saw a dream and visions in *his mind as he lay on his bed; then he wrote the dream down...."*) and Genesis 37:5–9 (Joseph had prophetic dreams about his future as a ruler to whom his brothers would bow down).

Prophetic dreams still occur today, just as the Lord said they would through the prophet Joel (quoted later in Acts 2 by Peter on the day of Pentecost): *"It will come about after this that I will pour out My Spirit on all mankind; and your sons and daughters will prophesy, your old men will dream dreams, your young men will see visions. Even on the male and female servants I will pour out My Spirit in those days"* (Joel 2:28–29).

The late John Paul Jackson of Streams Ministries was one of the best of the best when it came to understanding dreams. There are many others today, such as Barbi Breathitt and Doug Addison. I believe that God is raising up a true prophetic company in this generation.

4. Through angelic visitations. We see an example of this form of prophetic communication in the first two verses of the book of Revelation:

The Revelation of Jesus Christ, which God gave Him to show to His bond-servants, the things which must soon take place; and He sent and communicated it by His angel to His bond-servant John, who testified to the word of God and to the testimony of Jesus Christ, even to all that he saw.   (Revelation 1:1–2)

Two additional examples are when an angel brought a word to the centurion Cornelius to urge him to invite Peter to come to his home (see Acts 10:1–7, 22), and when an angel went to Paul aboard the storm-buffeted ship to reassure him that he and everyone else on that ship would be preserved, a message Paul communicated to the frightened sailors (see Acts 27:23–26).

HOW TO RELEASE PROPHETIC WORDS

Prophetic words can be released or expressed in a variety of wonderful ways: (1) by simple speech, (2) through prophetic gestures and actions, (3) in writing, (4) through song, or accompanied by musical instruments, and (5) through any number of other creative art forms.

1. *By simple speech.* The prophet talks to a group of people or to an individual to communicate the prophetic word. (See, for example, 1 Corinthians 14:4, 6, 19.) One of my friends was not a great platform preacher; instead, he was a "marketplace conversationalist" who released consistent prophetic insight to those with whom he spoke. We need more of this in order to reach all of the spheres of society.

2. *Through prophetic gestures and actions.* A good example of this is what the prophet Agabus did to warn Paul about what would happen when he went to Jerusalem. (See Acts 21:10–11.) For two other examples, see 1 Samuel 15:26–28 and Ezekiel 4.

3. *In writing.* I often write down a prophetic word so that people can "run with it." The Lord told the prophet Habakkuk, *"Record the vision and inscribe it on tablets, that the one who reads it may run"* (Habakkuk 2:2). Habakkuk used a stylus and clay tablets instead of a computer, a blog, or MP3s, but the idea is the same. Writing out a word provides a means for asking someone for confirmation and discernment if you're not quite sure about a word, and it is a simple, basic way of recording what the Lord has said.

Two other examples of the Lord commanding His prophets to record prophetic words are found in Jeremiah 36:1–3, where Jeremiah was instructed to write down the words he had received, and in Revelation 1:10–11, where John was instructed to write down the extensive vision that we know as the book of Revelation.

4. *Through song, or accompanied by musical instruments.* There is something about music that releases prophetic inspiration. Even seasoned prophets such as Elisha relied upon it: *"Elisha said, '…But now bring me a minstrel.' And it came about, when the minstrel played, that the hand of the* Lord *came upon [Elisha]"* (2 Kings 3:14–15). In another example, *"David and the commanders of the army set apart for the service some of the sons of Asaph and of Heman and of Jeduthun, who were to prophesy with lyres, harps and cymbals"* (1 Chronicles 25:1). In the New Testament, Paul encouraged the believers, *"Let the word of Christ richly dwell within you, with all wisdom teaching and admonishing one another with psalms and hymns and spiritual songs"* (Colossians 3:16; see also Ephesians 5:19). In our day, we have

pastors and prophetic preachers who are skilled musicians and who receive some of their clearest messages while singing or playing the piano, such as Kim Clement, Joseph Garlington, Julie Meyer, and even James Goll (!).

5. Through any number of other creative art forms. This way of communicating a prophetic word has been rediscovered in the modern church. It is no longer startling to see prophetic dancers, prophetic drama, or prophetic painting in the midst of a worship celebration. The dancers, actors, and artists lean into the Holy Spirit for inspiration, and they release "words" that are like dynamic, unfolding visions.

Sometimes, prophetic words are used more like "flavoring" in a sermon or another form of sharing, in a counseling session, or in intercessory prayer. Often, the person who speaks such words does not distinguish them from the context in which they are delivered. Regardless of the packaging, the Holy Spirit expresses Himself in a way that can benefit the hearers and gain the desired results.

Should every prophetic word find expression? I don't think so. Some words are "too hot to handle" and should be filed away for manifestation at a later time, pending confirmation and fine-tuning. I have personally prayed over certain words for more than fifteen years before I have felt I had permission to release them to the person they concerned. In world events today, some things are just now coming to pass that were spoken to me way back in 1987. So, I know that patience, part of the fruit of the Spirit, has its reward, as well!

Other words are simply too personal to convey; they are between you and the Lord, who speaks to you as a Friend. Like Mary, treasure such words in your heart and let them help you to follow your Shepherd more closely. (See Luke 2:19.)

MATURING IN THE GIFT OF PROPHECY

As with the other gifts of the Spirit, the gift of prophecy is not limited to functioning within the gathered assembly of believers, where someone might stand up behind a microphone and speak out a word from God. All of us with the prophetic gift have learned from experience, "testing the waters" in different situations as we mature in the gift, learning to stay alert for the word of the Lord and discovering where God can best use us.

Some people will hear Him best when they are alone in prayer, and a good number of those will be instructed in how to intercede based on the revelations they have received. Others will speak out in the context of prayer groups or in prayer counseling sessions. Some intercessors will find that the gift flows as they are prayer-walking, while others will learn to hear God's direction for evangelistic outreach. (Think about how that worked with Jesus and the Samaritan woman in John 4:4–40.)

With regard to maturing in the gift of prophecy, let us recognize that there are four categories of prophetic revelation: the *spirit* of prophecy, the *gift* of prophecy, the *ministry* of prophecy, and the *office* of a prophet. It is important to understand how they are distinct and how each has its place.

The Spirit of Prophecy

First, the spirit of prophecy refers to those occasions when the Spirit of God encompasses a group of people in what you could call a glory realm. God manifests His presence in the midst of the assembly in such a way that anybody can prophesy, whether or not they otherwise claim to have a gift of prophecy. We see the spirit of prophecy in Scripture in the story of King Saul:

> *Then Saul sent messengers to take David, but when they saw the company of the prophets prophesying, with Samuel standing and presiding over them, the Spirit of God came upon the messengers of Saul; and they also prophesied. When it was told Saul, he sent other messengers, and they also prophesied. So Saul sent messengers again the third time, and they also prophesied.* (1 Samuel 19:20–21)

The Gift of Prophecy

Second, the gift of prophecy, which we have been focusing on in this chapter, is the spiritual gift that God gives generously to His people in order to build them up and to help them walk with sure steps of faith. (Refer again to 1 Corinthians 12:10; 14:6, 24, 31.)

The Ministry of Prophecy

Third, people who exercise the gift of prophecy consistently over time have a ministry of prophecy, developing what you could term a "residential" gift, a ministry that is not circumstantial or occasional.

The Office of a Prophet

Beyond the ministry of prophecy is the office of a prophet (or prophetess). Such prophets are the ones who should carry the title "prophet," in my opinion. For glimpses of how they operated in the New Testament church, see Acts 13:1–3; 15:32; 21:10–11; 1 Corinthians 12:28–29; Ephesians 2:18–22; 3:4–6; 4:11–13. In many ways, they are like the Old Testament prophets who collected "schools" of other prophets around them.

Those in the office of prophet are equippers; they can tell others how the gift works. Lots of people who prophesy can't be considered equippers because they couldn't tell you how the gift works—they just do it (some of them brilliantly). People in the office of prophet are like spiritual fathers or mothers or equippers, whose emphasis (besides broadcasting the words God gives them) is on multiplication. They teach and model a prophetic lifestyle. They have earned the credibility and the authority to give direction and correction to those who operate in the basic prophetic functions of edification, exhortation, and comfort.

In 1 Corinthians 12:28, where it says that *"God has appointed in the church, first apostles, second **prophets**, third teachers, then miracles, then gifts of healings, helps, administrations, various kinds of tongues,"* it is the office of prophet that is being referred to. The office of prophet is paired with the apostolic office (see Ephesians 2:20; 3:5); such prophets' level of maturity and authority matches that of apostles (not particularly that of pastors, because pastors have authority over only one local church). Apostles are builders, as are those who operate in the office of prophet. This is why, when a known prophet (someone with the ministry but not the office) comes into a local assembly, he or she should not usurp the authority of the pastor but instead respect the given boundaries, functioning as one who blesses and encourages, not as one who gives divine directions and corrections.

In other words, there is a difference between revelation and authority. You can receive prophetic revelation, but that does not authorize you to direct decisions within the body. Unless you have been recognized as functioning in the office of prophet, you will lack not only the spiritual authority but also the wisdom for interpreting and applying the word of the Lord. It does not mean you are incorrect in what you have received; it just means that you may not be positioned to do as much with it as you would be if you had matured to the office of prophet. (This is not to say, however, that everyone who has been given a gift of prophecy will end up occupying the office of prophet, any more than every pastor will develop into an apostle. It depends on one's calling.)

Bottom line: God uses all of the prophetic variety in order to speak to His people in every situation. He uses not only the office of prophecy but also the spirit of prophecy, the gift of prophecy, and the ministry of prophecy.

RELEASING THE TESTIMONY OF JESUS

Ultimately, this is what all prophecy is about: releasing the testimony of Jesus. Here is John's visionary picture from the book of Revelation:

> Then I [John] fell at his [the angel's] feet to worship him. But he said to me, "Do not do that; I am a fellow servant of yours and your brethren who hold the testimony of Jesus; worship God. For **the testimony of Jesus is the spirit of prophecy.**" (Revelation 19:10)

Jesus wants to testify, and He uses men and women to do it. Those who serve as His voice do not draw attention to themselves but rather to the message and to the Messenger, the Holy Spirit. Whether the prophecy concerns momentous upcoming events or simple reassurance (such as "Do not fear!"), it releases the testimony of the Lamb who was slain and who now sits at the right hand of the Father.

Yes, the testimony of Jesus is released through the spirit of prophecy. And I am here to say that none of the gifts of the Holy Spirit have ceased. If you know where to look, you can attest to the fact that they are being released in our day in an unprecedented manner. I am so grateful for a new generation of both leaders and everyday believers who are moving in the revelatory gifts, the power gifts, and the vocal gifts of the Holy Spirit. Todd White, who was among those featured in the documentary *Holy Ghost* by Darren Wilson, is being used to raise the bar and call forth prophetic evangelists in our day. My sons in the faith, Matt Sorger, Steven Springer, and Munday Martin, along with many others, are flowing with great ease in the realms of the prophetic and the supernatural. It is a new day! But the gifts of the Spirit are not for the elite few; they are for every believer today!

Thank You, Lord, for pouring out Your Holy Spirit today! I am so grateful to be alive at this time in church history. Give me more opportunities to release the fragrance of Jesus everywhere I go and to encourage and comfort others through the gift of prophecy. Come, Holy Spirit, more powerfully in my life and in the lives of my family members. In Your love, empower us with Your revelatory gifts, for the sake of Your kingdom. Praise the Lord! Amen!

CLOSING EXHORTATION: FULFILLING THE GREAT COMMISSION TODAY

"Go therefore and make disciples of all the nations, baptizing them in the name of the Father and the Son and the Holy Spirit, teaching them to observe all that I commended you; and lo, I am with you always, even to the end of the age."
—Matthew 28:19–20

People's last words are very important. They are often sharing the one thing that burns in them the most so that it will leave a lasting impression on others. I know. The last word I received from my late my wife, Michal Ann Goll, came in a card (delivered by an angel on her behalf!) that stated, "Never, never, never, never give up!" I carry that card with those piercing words in its blue envelope in my Bible all around the world. Those words still echo in my being these many years later.

How much more should we take the last recorded words of Jesus from Matthew 28:19–20, given above, and have them burn in our own hearts and be the motivation for our lives today! We should also consider these words recorded in Scripture: *"Jesus Christ is the same yesterday and today and forever"* (Hebrews 13:8). This verse does not say anything even close to the following statements, which many people seem to think Jesus is saying to us: "What I did yesterday is good enough. It is written down for you to read. I did it then, but sorry, guys, I do not do that stuff anymore. You just get to read about those great times!"

To the contrary, Jesus declared bold statements that would be hard to exaggerate, such as *"Truly, truly, I say to you, he who believes in Me, the works that I do, he will do also; and greater works than these he will do; because I go to the Father."* I did not make that up. It comes from John 14:12 in the New Testament. It is not a line from a futuristic screenplay about an imaginary great adventure. These are the words of Jesus. He is waiting for us to believe Him so that we can do those *"greater works"*—today!

I have a dream in my heart. I want to see the entire global body of Christ—those who believe that the words of Jesus are true and for today—to arise empowered by the Holy Spirit to "do the stuff"! Not to be famous (give me a break!), and not to have their names in lights, but to do the works of Jesus so that the fame of His name may be spread far and wide and so the glory of the Lord will cover the earth as the waters cover the sea. (See Habakkuk 2:14.) Is my dream too big? Well, I did not make it up, either, because it is God's dream!

I opened this book with a short preface called "Just Do It!" Now I am closing the book with a short exhortation, "Fulfilling the Great Commission Today." How will the life and message of Jesus Christ have a chance to make an impact on every nation and people group on the face of the earth? How will the world's people truly be changed and discipled? By reading merely about things God did in the past? Is His name "Jehovah 'Was-y'"? Did God reveal Himself as the great "I Was"? I don't think so. He is the great I Am!

Enter into the adventure of your life by receiving and releasing the gifts of the Holy Spirit today! Be empowered for Jesus Christ's sake to make a permanent impact on the world around you by word and by deed with the great, great, great love of God. You have been commissioned to do the works of Jesus through the full operation of all the gifts of the Spirit—today! Blessings to each of you, my fellow laborers.

Now let me pray for you.

Father, as we close this study about the gifts of Your Holy Spirit, inspire each believer with the message of hope that his or her life matters. Bring divine appointments to these friends who have read this book. Lord, may You be magnified in all we do and say. Let the fragrance of Christ be released through our lives and impact all of our family members. Empower us as never before so that Jesus Christ will receive the rewards for His suffering. We thank You for the days in which we live, and we declare, "The best is yet to come!"

Amen!

—James W. Goll

NOTES

Chapter 1: What Are the Spiritual Gifts?

1. John Wimber, "Signs and Wonders, MC510," audio teaching based on a class taught for Fuller Theological Seminary (Anaheim, CA: Vineyard Ministries International, 1985).

2. The concept of the "dancing hand of God" is mainly a symbolic reference to the spontaneous activity of the Holy Spirit where He moves upon different individuals in a particular manner and anoints or empowers them with a grace or gift for that specific situation or gathering. He "lands," or "falls," upon the gathered believers and supernaturally enables different ones to function in, receive, and release various giftings.

3. Wimber, "Signs and Wonders," (quoting Mel Robeck), emphasis mine.

4. Dick Iverson, *The Holy Spirit Today* (Portland, OR: City Christian Publishing, 2006), 75.

5. C. Peter Wagner, *Discover Your Spiritual Gifts* (Ventura, CA: Regal Books, 2005), 20.

6. Ibid., 21–22.

7. Derek Prince, *The Gifts of the Spirit* (New Kensington, PA: Whitaker House, 2007), 20.

Chapter 4: The Gift of Discerning of Spirits

1. See Kenneth Hagin, *The Holy Spirit and His Gifts* (Tulsa, OK: Kenneth Hagin Ministries, 1991), 109–111.

2. Iverson, *Holy Spirit Today*, 125.
3. David Pytches, *Spiritual Gifts in the Local Church* (Minneapolis, MN: Bethany House, 1985), 87.
4. Sam Storms, *The Beginner's Guide to Spiritual Gifts* (Minneapolis, MN: Bethany House, 2012), 131.

Chapter 5: The Gift of a Word of Wisdom

1. Prince, *Gifts of the Spirit*, 53.
2. Storms, *Beginner's Guide*, 46.
3. Iverson, *Holy Spirit Today*, 106.
4. Wimber, "Signs and Wonders."
5. The gifts of the Spirit are like the colors of the rainbow, blending together as needed to achieve the end result. Here the gifts of discerning of spirits and wisdom blend seamlessly. I will discuss this concept further in chapter 6.

Chapter 6: The Gift of a Word of Knowledge

1. Storms, *Beginner's Guide*, 49, emphasis mine.
2. Wagner, *Discover Your Spiritual Gifts*, 110. My addition in brackets.
3. Prince, *Gifts of the Spirit*, 73.
4. Wimber, "Signs and Wonders."
5. Pytches, *Spiritual Gifts*, 99.
6. James W. Goll, et al., *Adventures in the Prophetic* (Shippensburg, PA: Destiny Image, 2010), 16–18. Emphasis is in original.

Chapter 7: The Gift of Faith

1. Hagin, *Holy Spirit and His Gifts*, 118, emphasis in the original.
2. Iverson, *Holy Spirit Today*, 131, emphasis in the original.
3. Pytches, *Spiritual Gifts*, 109.
4. Lester Sumrall, *The Gifts and Ministries of the Holy Spirit* [updated edition] (New Kensington, PA: Whitaker House, 1982), 96–97.
5. From the song "More Love, More Power" by Jude Del Hierro.

Chapter 8: The Gifts of Healings

1. Storms, *Beginner's Guide*, 69.
2. Prince, *Gifts of the Spirit*, 128.
3. Ibid., 129.
4. Hagin, *Holy Spirit and His Gifts*, 133.
5. Wimber, "Signs and Wonders."

Chapter 9: The Workings of Miracles

1. Storms, *Beginner's Guide*, 88.
2. Iverson, *Holy Spirit Today*, 151.
3. Wayne Grudem, quoted in Storms, *Beginner's Guide*, 88.

Chapter 10: The Gift of Various Kinds of Tongues

1. Hagin, *Holy Spirit and His Gifts*, 149.
2. Storms, *Beginner's Guide*, 162.
3. Ibid., 156.

Chapter 11: The Gift of Interpretation of Tongues

1. Prince, *Gifts of the Spirit*, 168.
2. Wimber, "Signs and Wonders"; Pytches, *Spiritual Gifts*, 73.
3. Hagin, *Holy Spirit and His Gifts*, 157.
4. Ibid.
5. Iverson, *Holy Spirit Today*, 175.
6. Storms, *Beginner's Guide*, 193.
7. See Prince, *Gifts of the Spirit*, 171–173.
8. *"If anyone speaks in a tongue, it should be by two or at the most three, and each in turn, and one must interpret; but if there is no interpreter, he must keep silent in the church; and let him speak to himself and to God. Let two or three prophets speak, and let the others pass judgment. But if a revelation is made to another who is seated, the first one must keep silent. For you can all prophesy one by one, so that all may learn and all may be exhorted; and the spirits of prophets are subject to prophets"* (1 Corinthians 14:27–32).

Chapter 12: The Gift of Prophecy

1. Storms, *Beginner's Guide*, 110.
2. Prince, *Gifts of the Spirit*, 182–83.
3. W. E. Vine, *Vine's Complete Expository Dictionary of Old and New Testament Words* (Nashville, TN: Thomas Nelson, Inc., Publishers, 1984, 1986), 492, Greek #4394. All rights reserved.
4. *Strong's Talking Greek and Hebrew Dictionary*, QuickVerse 10, Hebrew #5012.
5. Wimber, "Signs and Wonders."
6. See, for example, Prince, *Gifts of the Spirit*, 203–222.
7. Ibid., 192.

RESOURCE MATERIALS

Bickle, Mike. *Growing in the Prophetic: A Practical, Biblical Guide to Dreams, Visions, and Spiritual Gifts*. Lake Mary, FL: Charisma House, 2008.

Chavda, Mahesh. *The Hidden Power of Healing Prayer*. Shippensburg, PA: Destiny Image, 2001.

Fortune, Don, and Katie Fortune. *Discover Your God-Given Gifts*. Grand Rapids, MI: Chosen Books, 2009.

Goll, James W. *Deliverance from Darkness: The Essential Guide to Defeating Demonic Strongholds and Oppression*. Grand Rapids, MI: Chosen Books, 2010.

———. *Living a Supernatural Life: The Secret to Experiencing a Life of Miracles* (formerly titled *The Beginner's Guide to Signs, Wonders and the Supernatural Life*). Ventura, CA: Regal Books, 2013.

———. *The Lifestyle of a Prophet: A 21-Day Journey to Embracing Your Calling*. Grand Rapids, MI: Chosen Books, 2013.

———. *The Prophetic Intercessor: Releasing God's Purposes to Change Lives and Influence Nations*. Grand Rapids, MI: Chosen Books, 2007.

———. *The Seer: The Prophetic Power of Visions, Dreams, and Open Heavens*. Rev. ed. Shippensburg, PA: Destiny Image, 2012.

Goll, James W. and Michal Ann Goll. *Angelic Encounters*. Lake Mary, FL: Charisma House, 2007.

———. *Dream Language: The Prophetic Power of Dreams, Revelations, and the Spirit of Wisdom*. Shippensburg, PA: Destiny Image, 2006.

Goll, James W., and Michal Ann Goll, Jeff Jansen, Patricia King, Mickey Robinson, Ryan Wyatt. *Adventures in the Prophetic*. Shippensburg, PA: Destiny Image, 2010.

Hagin, Kenneth. *The Holy Spirit and His Gifts*. 2nd ed. Tulsa, OK: Kenneth Hagin Ministries, 1991.

Ireland, David. *Activating the Gifts of the Holy Spirit*. New Kensington, PA: Whitaker House, 1998.

Iverson, Dick. *The Holy Spirit Today*. Portland, OR: City Bible Publishing, 2006.

Johnson, Bill, and Randy Clark. *The Essential Guide to Healing*. Grand Rapids, MI: Chosen Books, 2011.

Prince, Derek. *The Gifts of the Spirit*. New Kensington, PA: Whitaker House, 2007.

Pytches, David. *Spiritual Gifts in the Local Church*. Minneapolis, MN: Bethany House, 1987.

Sandford, John, and Paula Sandford. *The Elijah Task*. Lake Mary, FL: Charisma House, 2006.

Storms, Sam. *The Beginner's Guide to Spiritual Gifts*. 2nd ed. Minneapolis, MN: Bethany House, 2012.

Sumrall, Lester. *Gifts and Ministries of the Holy Spirit*. New Kensington, PA: Whitaker House, 2005.

Wagner, C. Peter. *Discover Your Spiritual Gifts*. Ventura, CA: Regal Books, 2005.

Wimber, John. "Signs & Wonders & Church Growth" (DVD). Stafford, TX: Vineyard Resources (recorded in the 1980s). (See http://www.vineyardresources.com/equip/.)

OTHER BOOKS BY JAMES W. GOLL

Passionate Pursuit

Prayer Storm

The Lost Art of Intercession

The Coming Israel Awakening

And many more...

In addition, there are numerous study guides available, including *Impacting the World Through Spiritual Gifts*, *Discovering the Seer in You*, *Exploring the Gift and Nature of Dreams*, *Prayer Storm*, *A Radical Faith*, *Prophetic Foundations*, *Walking in the Supernatural Life*, and many others with corresponding CD and MP3 albums and DVD messages.

ABOUT THE AUTHOR

James W. Goll is a lover of Jesus who cofounded Encounters Network, which is dedicated to changing lives and impacting nations by releasing God's presence through prophetic, intercessory, and compassionate ministry. James is the director of Prayer Storm, a 24/7/365 media-based house of prayer. He is also the founder of the God Encounters Training e-School of the Heart—where faith and life meet.

After pastoring in the Midwest, James was thrust into the role of an equipper and trainer internationally. He has traveled extensively to every continent, carrying a passion for Jesus wherever he goes. He is a member of the Harvest International Ministry apostolic team and a consultant to ministries around the world. James desires to see the body of Christ become the house of prayer for all nations and be empowered by the Holy Spirit to spread the good news to every country and to all peoples. He is the author of numerous books and training manuals, and he is a contributing writer for several periodicals.

James and Michal Ann Goll were married for more than 32 years before her graduation to heaven in the fall of 2008. They have four wonderful adult children, all of whom are now married; and James is now "Gramps" to three adorable grandchildren. He makes his home amongst the southern charm of Franklin, Tennessee, and continues in his passionate pursuit of the Lover of his soul.

For more information:

James W. Goll
Encounters Network
P.O. Box 1653
Franklin, TN 37065

www.encountersnetwork.com • www.prayerstorm.com
www.compassionacts.com • www.GETeSchool.com
info@encountersnetwork.com *or* inviteJames@gmail.com

COMPASSION ACTS
love taking action

Compassion Acts was founded by Michal Ann Goll in 2004 as a ministry and humanitarian aid organization to provide help for those in need. Even though she is no longer with us today, we still carry on the heart and soul of Compassion Acts in her stead. Today, Compassion Acts operates in a pursuit of justice, disaster relief and humanitarian aid work in response to Michal Ann's personal charge found in her last will and testament.

CA EFFORTS AROUND THE WORLD

Mission Projects -
sending resources and volunteers to help meet specific needs

Emergency Relief -
responding to natural disasters through rice shipments and humanitarian aid

Project Dreamers Park -
building playgrounds and community centers to inspire children to dream

First Nations in America -
serving Native Americans by providing food, health supplies and education

Want to Get Involved? Find out More at:
COMPASSIONACTS.COM

 **The Hour That Changes The World**

Releasing the Global Moravian Lampstand

"Fire shall be kept Burning continually on the altar; it is not to go out."

-LEVITICUS 6:13

The Vision of PrayerStorm is to restore and release the Moravian model of the watch of the Lord into homes and prayer rooms around the world.

Web based teaching, prayer bulletins, and resources are utilized to facilitate round-the-clock worship and prayer to win for the Lord the rewards of His suffering!

Hourly worship and prayer around the world will be maintained with four primary emphases:

REVIVAL IN THE CHURCH

PRAYER FOR ISRAEL

WORLD'S GREATEST YOUTH AWAKENING

CRISIS INTERVENTION THROUGH INTERCESSION

GOVERNMENTAL INTERCESSION

Find out More at:
PrayerStorm.com